Sphinx Theatre Company presents

CHERISHED DISAPPOINTMENTS IN LOVE

a play

by **Jouko** and **Juha Turkka**
adapted from the Finnish by **Bryony Lavery**
literal translation by Kaarina Kytömaa

The original play premiered at Tampere Workers' Theatre,
Finland on 24 January 1996

The English adaptation was first performed at the Soho Theatre
on 12 September 2001

Sphinx Theatre Company is sponsored by Gander & White

Sphinx Theatre Company Regd. Charity No: 279627
Soho Theatre Company Regd. Charity No: 267234

THE
ARTS
COUNCIL
OF ENGLAND

sphinx

• soho
• theatre company

CHERISHED DISAPPOINTMENTS IN LOVE
by **Jouko** and **Juha Turkka**

Elsa	Janet Suzman
Sergeant-Major	Les Dennis
Himanen	Esa-Matti Pölhö
Kate	Nicky Ladanowski

Director	Sue Parrish
Adapter	Bryony Lavery
Designer	Liz Cooke
Assistant to Designer	Naomi Reed
Lighting Designer	Bruno Poet
Sound Designer	Alison Dale
Staff Director	Claire Russ
Fight Director	Terry King
Stage Manager	Paul Daintry
Deputy Stage Manager	Louise Balhatchet

Sphinx would like to thank the following people and organisations for their generous help and support in the development of this work:

Pirjo Westmann and the Finnish Dramatists' Union, the Information Centre for Finnish Literature, Paulina Ahokas and the Finnish Institute in London, Sickan Park, Anna-Maria Liukko, Jussi Helminen, Francis Alexander, Louis Hilyer, Gabrielle Jourdan, Jonathan Oliver, Ben Porter, Abigail Thaw, Nonnie Creagh-Brown, Alison Ritchie, Colonel Peter Dick Peter, Number Seven Company Coldstream Guards, The Young Vic Theatre.

Janet Suzman, Elsa

Janet Suzman came to the UK from South Africa, and after training at LAMDA joined the RSC for their quarter-centenary history cycle, *The Wars of the Roses*. Other Stratford roles include: Katharina, Beatrice, Rosalind, Berinthia, Lavinia, Cleopatra. London roles include: *The Three Sisters* (Evening Standard Award), *Hedda Gabler,* Fugard's *Hello and Goodbye* (Evening Standard Award), *The Good Woman of Setzuan*, *Another Time*, *The Sisters Rosenweig*.

Directing credits include: *Othello* for the Market Theatre, South Africa and Channel 4; *A Dream of People* for the RSC, *Death of a Salesman* for Theatr Clwyd (Liverpool Echo Production Award); her own Africanised version of Brecht's play, renamed *The Good Woman of Sharkville* for The Market and West Yorkshire Playhouse, and *The Free State – a South African Response to The Cherry Orchard* for Birmingham Repertory Theatre (Barclays TMA Best Director Award). The play is published by Methuen.

Janet directed Sphinx Theatre Company's production of *The Snow Palace* by Pam Gems, which played at the Tricycle Theatre and toured Poland (nominated for the TMA / Barclays award for Best Touring Production).

Les Dennis, Sergeant-Major

Recent theatre work includes: *Misery* (Coliseum, Oldham); *Chicago* (West End); *Mr Wonderful* (Gateway, Chester); *Skylight* (Watermill, Newbury); *Don't Dress for Dinner* (National Tour); *Me and My Girl* (West End).

TV: *Family Fortunes* (Carlton); *Brookside* (Channel 4); *Doctors, Happy Birthday Shakespeare, Bang Bang it's Reeves and Mortimer* (all BBC); *The Grimleys* (Carlton); *Wyrd Sisters* (Channel 4); *Family Affairs* (Channel 5).

Radio: *Bob Gives Up His Day Job, Like They've Never Been Gone* (Radio 4).

Film: *Intimate Relations*.

Esa-Matti Pölhö, Himanen

Trained: *Theatre Academy of Finland.*

Theatre: *Family Stories; Living and Dead Ones* (Group Theatre)*; Godot; Hamlet; Woyzeck; Pterodactyls; Seven Brothers; Equus; Kalevala* (all for the Finnish National Theatre); *Peer Gynt; In the Bottom* (Theatre Jurkka).

TV: *Secret Lives* (Pearson); *Great Game, High Stakes* (YLE); *Wasp's Struggle* (Kroma); *Wonderful Man, Under the Starlamp* (Solar).

Nicky Ladanowski, Kate

Theatre: *Vanity Fair* (Chester Gateway); *Death of a Salesman* (Royal National Theatre).

TV: *Holby City* (BBC); *Coronation Street* (Granada); *The Bill* (3-parter; Pearson); *People like Us* and *Jonathan Creek* (BBC).

Film: *The Waiting Game; Appetite; Poppy's Present; Apart; Girl* .

Liz Cooke, Designer

Liz Cooke trained at the Slade Schools of Fine Art and Oxford University.

Theatre credits include: *The Magic Toyshop* (Shared Experience); *Les Blancs* (Royal Exchange, Manchester); *The Hackney Office* and *The Spirit of Annie Ross* (Druid Theatre Company); *The Daughter in Law* (Orange Tree, Richmond); *The Beauty Queen of Leenane* (Salisbury Playhouse); *The Gift* (Birmingham Repertory Theatre); *Better* (BAC); *Spoonface Steinberg* (New Ambassador's Theatre and Sheffield Crucible); *Cooking with Elvis* (Live Theatre, Newcastle and Whitehall Theatre); *The Comedy of Errors* (Shakespeare's Globe); *The Glory of Living* (Royal Court Upstairs); *The Idiot* (West Yorkshire Playhouse and Tour); *Volunteers* (Gate Theatre); *The Promise* and *Arabian Nights: The Tales of Scherazade* (BAC); *A Time of Fire* (Birmingham Repertory Theatre).

Opera credits include: *Carmen, Don Giovanni, La Traviata* (Holland Park Festival); *Tosca* (European Chamber Opera).

Alison Dale, Sound Designer

Alison Dale's sound career began in 1990 at the Royal Exchange Theatre in Manchester after which in 1992 she joined the Sound Department at the West Yorkshire Playhouse, where she operated and designed many shows over a three year period. Since becoming Freelance her shows have included *Five Guys named Moe* as sound Engineer, *Phantom of the Opera* UK National Tour, Stadschouwberg Antwerp and Det Ny Theater Copenhagen as Assistant Sound Designer, and as Associate Sound Designer *Jekyll and Hyde* in Bremen and *Beauty and the Beast* in London, Stuttgart, and on UK National Tour.

Alison has worked extensively with Autograph Sound Recording on projects as diverse as the *Marriage of Figaro* televised on the BBC's live music day and Andrew Lloyd Webbers' 50th Birthday celebration at the Albert Hall.

Bryony Lavery, Adapter

A rounded theatre practitioner, Bryony Lavery's skills extend to performer (most notably as Tinkerbell in *Peter Pan* at the Drill Hall), artistic director (Gay Sweatshop and Female Trouble), writer of children's theatre (including *The Dragon Wakes, Madagascar* and *Down Among the Mini Beast*) and of many cabarets (including *Floorshow* with Caryl Churchill for Monstrous Regiment in 1977). From 1989 to 1992 she was Tutor-Lecturer on the M.A. Playwriting Course at Birmingham University.

Bryony Lavery's plays include *Helen and Her Friends* (1978); *Bag* (1979); *The Family Album* (1980); *Calamity* (1983); *Origin of the Species* (1984); *Witchcraze* (1985); *Her Aching Heart* (Pink Paper Play of the Year Award 1991); *Kitchen Matters* (1990); *Nothing Compares to You* (1995); *Ophelia* (1996); *Frozen* (which won both the TMA Best New Play 1998 and the Eileen Anderson Central Television Award for Best Play); an adaptation of Kate Atkinson's *Behind the Scenes at the Museum* (2000).

Bryony has recently completed *Easter* for Birmingham Repertory Theatre, and is currently working on *Smoke*, commissioned by the New Vic Theatre, Stoke on Trent.

Recent plays for Sphinx Theatre Company include *Goliath*, based upon Beatrix Campbell's book, and *A Wedding Story*, which is currently touring nationally. Her adaptation of Angela Carter's *The Magic Toyshop* has recently been produced by Shared Experience and is touring nationally.

Bryony is an honorary Doctor of Arts of De Montfort University.

Sue Parrish, Director

Sue Parrish has been Artistic Director of Sphinx Theatre Company since 1990. Trained as a ballet dancer, Sue graduated from University College London with a B.A.Hons. She began her theatre career as an Arts Council Trainee Director at the Half Moon Theatre in London, has run her own company and was appointed Associate Director at Greenwich Theatre 1989/90. She is the current Chair of the Theatre Committee at the Directors Guild of Great Britain.

Most recent directing credits include: as Assistant Director to Mike Alfreds for Shared Experience's *A Handful of Dust, Cider with Rosie; Can't Pay, Won't Pay* by Dario Fo; *The Way of The World* by Congreve; *The Provok'd Wife* by Vanbrugh; *Hamlet, Playhouse Creatures* by April de Angelis; *Black Sail,White Sail* by Helene Cixous; *Hanjo* by Seami and Mishima; *Voyage In The Dark* by Jean Rhys; *Sweet Dreams* by Diane Esguerra.

Music Theatre Direction for the City of London Festival in the Guildhall Great Hall: *A Midsummer Night's Dream* with incidental music by Mendelssohn, with the Orchestra of the Age of Enlightenment conducted by Paul Daniel (1997); *The Tempest* with incidental music by Purcell and contemporaries, with the Orchestra of the Musicians of The Globe conducted by Philip Pickett (1998); *Hamlet* with incidental music by Tchaikovsky, Prokofiev and Shostakovich, with the Academy of St.Martin in the Fields conducted by Sir Neville Marriner (2000).

As producer Sue has produced all of Sphinx's recent national and international tours, as well as the Company's major Glass Ceiling conferences, held at the National Theatre since 1991.

Bruno Poet, Lighting Designer

Credits include: *Les Blancs* (Manchester Royal Exchange); Garsington Opera 1998-2001; The National Opera Studio Showcase (QEH); *The External* (Bath Theatre Royal/Tour); *Neville's Island* (Watford Palace); *Love's Labours Lost* and *The Cherry Orchard* (English Touring Theatre); *The Lodger* (Windsor/ Bromley); *Orfeo et Euridice* (Opera National du Rhin / Teatro Calderon de Valladlid / Festival Mozart de La Coruna); *Norma* (Gran Teatro del Liceu Barcelona); *Musik* (Plymouth Theatre Royal); *Al Murray: The Pub Landlord* (Playhouse Theatre); *The Turn of the Screw* (Brighton Festival); *Much Ado About Nothing* (Guildhall School); *Pleasure Palaces* and *Hansel and Gretel* (Lyric Hammersmith) and *Tess of the D'Urbervilles* (Savoy).

Future productions include: *Macbeth* (Jutland Opera); *So Long Life* (Theatre Royal Bath / Tour); *The Homecoming* (Royal Exchange); *Sexual Perversity in Chicago, The Shawl* and *The Birthday Party* (Crucible, Sheffield), and *Yeomen of the Guard* for British Youth Opera.

Claire Russ, Staff Director

Claire Russ graduated from the Laban Centre for Movement and Dance. After training in Graham technique, Ballet, Contact Improvisation and Release technique she has developed her own style of technical and theatrical movement with further influence from Japanese and Chinese movement forms and other Expressionistic dance styles.

The Claire Russ Ensemble was established in 1990, and has been touring successfully throughout Britain. Previous Ensemble productions include: *Dangerous When Wet (1995/6)* – inspired bu the world of Busby Berkley; *Sweet Boys (1996/7)*; *Gourmet (1997/8) and (B&B)*. The ensemble has recently been touring its most recent work – *veilSAFE*; a new interactive dance and visual art performance. Claire is currently developing a new site-sensitive performance project – LIVEspace – conceived of for creation and performance in new architectural environments.

Alongside her work for the Ensemble, Claire undertakes a full range of commissions and projects. Recent projects include working with Sphinx Theatre Company on their new production *Sweet Dreams;* a commission from Foreign Bodies Dance Company in Northampton, – *Four Square Place* based on Michele Roberts' book Impossible Saints'; and *Accidental Damage* – a dance film commissioned by Staffordshire Arts & Museums Service created together with women who were victims of domestic violence.

Jouko Turkka, Writer

Jouko Turkka is one of Finland's most prolific and widely-respected theatre writers and directors. Apart from his several plays he has also published novels and written for the television and radio. Between 1981 and 1988 he was a lecturer in Drama at the University of Helsinki.

Outi Nyytäjä writes about Turkka's theatre that: 'as a director and dramatist (he) is one of the leading personalities and without doubt the most controversial one of the Finnish theatre… Turkka's Finnish are Southlanders. They react quickly; the men are wild and tender, the women self-confident and ecstatic. Turkka has created a complete category of beauties and men-eaters'.

SPHINX THEATRE COMPANY

Sphinx has played a proud and historic role in British theatre over the past 27 years. Supported by the Arts Council of England since 1975, it has toured nationally and internationally, specialising in producing new work by established women artists. There is scarcely a woman writer working in the theatre today who has not worked with the company, or who has not been touched by its pioneering activities.

Most recent productions:

Sweet Dreams by Diane Esguerra, a dramatic interpretation of Freud's Case Study of Dora.

Sweet Dreams was first produced in association with the Chelsea Centre, London in October 1999, and the production then toured England in May – June 2000. This provocative play generated huge interest from critics and audiences alike. Sphinx also organised a series of debates to coincide with the production, in which prominent psychoanalysts and academics put 'Freud on the Couch'.

A Wedding Story by Bryony Lavery.

A Wedding Story was first co-produced with Birmingham Repertory Theatre, and opened at the Door, Birmingham Rep in November 2000 before transferring to the Soho Theatre for a sell-out run in January 2001. Sphinx are now touring nationally their production of this brilliant new play.

A Wedding Story will be playing at Greenwich Theatre from the 25 – 29 September 2001. Box office 020 8858 7755

Commissioned writers: Pam Gems, Claire Luckham, Timberlake Wertenbaker, Sheila White

Artistic Director:	Sue Parrish
General Manager:	Amanda Rigali
Associate Producer:	Mark Slaughter
Production Manager:	Paul Hennessy @ Background
Press Representative:	Bridget Thornborrow 020 7247 4437

Sphinx Theatre Company
25 Short St
London SE1 8LJ
0207 401 9993
www.sphinxtheatre.co.uk

SPHINX PAST PRODUCTIONS

1973   *Instrument for Love* by Jennifer Phillips
The Amiable Courtship of Miz Venus and Wild Bill by Pam Gems
Lovefood by Dinah Brook
Mal de Mere by Micheline Wandor
Parade of Cats by Jane Wibberly

1974   *Fantasia* by the company

1975/6 *My Mother Says I Never Should* by the company

1976/7 *Work to Role* by the Company
Out on the Costa del Trico by the company

1977/8 *Pretty Ugly* by the company
In Our Way by the company

1978/9 *Hot Spot* by Eileen Fairweather and Melissa Murray
Soap Opera by Donna Franceschild

1979/80 *The Wild Bunch* by Bryony Lavery
My Mkinga by the company

1980/1 *Better a Live Pompey than a Dead Cyril* by Claire McIntyre and Stephanie Nunn
Breaking Through by Timberlake Wertenbaker

1981   *New Anatomies* by Timberlake Wertenbaker1982
Time Pieces by Lou Wakefield and the company
Double Vision by Libby Mason1983
Love and Dissent by Elisabeth Bond
Dear Girl by Libby Mason and Tierl Thompson

1984   *Trade Secrets* by Jacqui Shapiro

1984/5 *Pax* by Deborah Levy

1985   *Anywhere to Anywhere* by Joyce Halliday
Witchcraze by Bryony Lavery

1986   *Fixed Deal* by Paulette Randall
Our Lady by Deborah Levy

1987   *Holding the Reins* by the company
Lear's Daughters by Elaine Feinstein, with the company
Picture Palace by Winsome Pinnock
Pinchdice & Co. by Julie Wilkinson
Zerri's Choice by Sandra Yaw
Mortal by Maro Green and Caroline Griffin
Her Aching Heart by Bryony Lavery

1990   *Christmas Without Herods* by Lisa Evans
The Roaring Girl's Hamlet by Shakespeare, in a setting by Claire Luckham

1992/3 *Every Bit Of It* by Jackie Kay

1993   *Playhouse Creatures* by April De Angelis

1994   *Chandralekha* by Amrit Wilson
Black Sail White Sail by Helene Cixous

1995   *Hanjo* by Seami, adapted by Diane Esguerra and Yukio Mishima, trans. Donald Keene

1996   *Voyage in the Dark* by Jean Rhys, adapted by Joan Wiles
Goliath by Bryony Lavery based on the book by Beatrix Campbell
Nichola McAuliffe nominated for TMA / Barclays Best Actress Award 1997
The Snow Palace by Pam Gems
Nominated for TMA / Barclays Best New Play Award 1998

1999   *Vita & Virginia* by Eileen Atkins, based on the correspondence of Virginia Woolf and Vita Sackville-West

1999/00 *Sweet Dreams* by Diane Esguerra

2000/01 *A Wedding Story* by Bryony Lavery

2001   *Cherished Disappointments in Love*, adapted from the Finnish by Bryony Lavery

GLASS CEILINGS
Sphinx's regular event about women in the arts.

1991 at the ICA with Professor Janet Todd, Dr Juliet Dusinberre, Sue Parrish (Chair); Fiona Shaw, Charlotte Keatley, Jill Tweedie and Jenni Murray (Chair).

1992 at the ICA with Hélène Cixous, Sarah Cornell, and Sue Parrish (Chair); Janet Suzman, Deborah Warner, Fiona Shaw, Jackie Kay, and Jenni Murray (Chair).

1993 at the Royal National Theatre with Beatrix Campbell, Susie Orbach and Sue Parrish (Chair); Jude Kelly (Chair), Hélène Cixous, Viv Gardner, Juliet Stephenson, Rona Munro and Di Trevis.

1994 at the Royal National Theatre with Helena Kennedy QC (Chair), Amrit Wilson, Taslima Nasrin and Irina Ratushinskaya; Ruth MacKenzie (Chair), Beatrix Campbell, Jude Kelly, Phyllis Nagy, and Judith Jacob.

1995 at the Royal National Theatre with Sarah Dunant (Chair), Professor Susan Bassnett and Della Grace; Ruth Mackenzie (Chair), Claire Armistead, Annie Castledine, Kay Mellor, Toyah Willcox and Denise Wong.

1996 at the Royal National Theatre with Germaine Greer, Juliet Mitchell and Dr Lizbeth Goodman (Chair); Jude Kelly (Chair), Annie Castlediine, Pam Gems, Bonnie Greer, Sarah Kane, and Mel Kenyon.

1997 at the Almeida Theatre with Professor Lisa Jardine, Joan Bakewell; Nicholas de Jongh, Mike Phillips, Genista McIntosh (Chair), Beatrix Campbell, Kathryn Hunter, Fiona Shaw, Desmond Barrit and Burt Caesar.

2001 at the Royal National Theatre with Beatrix Campbell; Nancy Lindisfarne; Professor Juliet Mitchell; Professor Laurence Senelick; Professor Sara Diamond; Helena Goldwater; Dr Lizbeth Goodman; Bonnie Greer and Bryony Lavery.

soho theatre

Soho Theatre and Writers' Centre
21 Dean Street, London W1D 3NE
Admin: 020 7287 5060 Fax: 020 7287 5061
Box Office: 020 7478 0100 minicom: 020 7478 0136
www.sohotheatre.com   email: mail@sohotheatre.com

Gordon's.

Bars and Restaurant
The main theatre bar is located in Café Lazeez Brasserie on the Ground
Floor. The Gordon's® Terrace serves Gordon's® Gin and Tonic and a
range of soft drinks and wine. Reservations for the Café Lazeez restaurant
can be made on 020 7434 9393.

Free Mailing List: Join our mailing list by contacting the Box Office on
020 7478 0100 or email us at mail@sohotheatre.com for regular online
information.

Hiring the theatre: Soho theatre has a range of rooms and spaces for
hire. Please contact the theatre managers on 020 7287 5060 or email
hires@sohotheatre.com for further details.

Soho Theatre Company

SOHO THEATRE DEVELOPMENT

Soho Theatre Company receives core funding from Westminster City Council and London Arts but in order to provide as diverse a programme as possible and expand our audience development and outreach work, we rely upon additional support. Many projects are only made possible by donations from trusts, foundations and individuals and corporate involvement.

stone

Gordon's.

Bloomberg

TBWA\GGT DIRECT

A&B Arts & Business

All our major sponsors share a common commitment to developing new areas of activity with the arts. We specifically encourage a creative partnership between Soho Theatre Company, the sponsors and their employees.

This translates into special ticket offers, creative writing workshops, innovative PR campaigns and hospitality events.

The **New Voices** annual membership scheme is for people who care about new writing and the future of theatre. There are various levels to suit all – for further information, please visit our website at:
www.sohotheatre.com/newvoices

Our new **Studio Seats** campaign is to raise money and support for the vital and unique work that goes on behind the scenes at Soho Theatre. Alongside reading and assessing over 2000 scripts a year, we also work intensively with writers through workshops, showcases, writers' discussion nights and rehearsed readings. For only £300 you can take a seat in the Education and Development Studio to support this crucial work.

If you would like to help, or have any questions, please contact the development department on 020 7287 5060 or at:
development@sohotheatre.com

We are grateful to all of our sponsors and donors for their support and commitment.

LONDON ARTS

SUPPORTED BY
CITY OF
WESTMINSTER

Author's Note

We are going to watch a production where *everything* has gone wrong from the start to the finish. The director/writer/ designers disagreed...many were not up to their job...there were rewrites which were worse than the first inadequate draft...the director ran a very bad rehearsal process in which the actors discussed and bickered instead of rehearsing...actors wrote and rewrote their own scenes and other scenes and proved themselves even worse writers than the writer. The design was cut, played about with, things were demanded willfully, then no place could be found for them. The crew gave up long ago, but are being paid nightly so just sling anything on. The lead actress...such a good idea as she seemed...got horribly confused by the director's way of working...and the rewriting...walked...after falling in love with the leading man...a young philosophy academic from Finland...who is playing himself...but he cannot act. The second female lead has tried womanfully to find motivation for every twist and turn of her underwritten character. The sergeant-major is a somewhat middle aged stage military man of uncertain temper, sanity and dimensions. There are vestiges of a huge design concept but always in the wrong place, delivered by a disaffected crew who are trying to operate a sound and lighting plan on cues which have long since vanished or been altered. There is a skeletal plot in there somewhere, which occasionally the actors follow...but mostly not. *Very occasionally*...an actor will act a bit. But mostly the lead actress is confused, indignant, in love, in despair, dying...and rarely acting. The sergeant-major is acting so hard he has forgotten he is a stage character. Himanen, the philosopher, has not the slightest idea what a stage is, or how to behave on it. Every single rule of good theatre is unsystematically, randomly, broken. There is no structure, shape or arc. This is a piece where *everybody* got *everything* Wrong...
It is Chaos. It is Life.

ACT ONE

Scene 1

The auditorium of a theatre. A play is about to start. The play is probably about a powerful woman newspaper editor…and the set suggests her expensive flat. There are various expensive scene changes, effects…which may occur at the wrong time. The play does not start. Instead a respected, revered actress of the Theatre, sitting in the front row of the audience, wearing some perturbing nightwear, starts speaking. She is not acting…

ELSA: Listen
    I'm sorry…
    I know you think
    I'm in this play.
    I'm not.
    I walked out *weeks* ago…
    and I'm someone who *never* walks out on a contract!
    despite the Director having asked for me rather than
    Maggie Smith… Diana Rigg… I mean
    Dames…
    But something spoke to me…
    something deep, deep inside here said…
    'Get Out, Run Like A Stag!'
    And now…
    I'm here as a mere *audience member…*
    because these *colleagues* backstage
    don't want me to see what's going on in this *performance*
    or whatever *Management* is calling this travesty!
    I had to get a friend of mine to
    buy me a ticket with *money…*my *own* money…I paid
    money
    to
    come to the theatre!

The shuddering horror of it…

    Darlings…for the first time in my long…my
    distinguished career…
    I asked for the support of my colleagues against the

director…
and they stuck with *her*!
I was really beginning to open myself up…to *unfold*
myself to a love…
The very place where a human being is most vulnerable
…where you can die from a wrong word…
where one look can make you collapse like an ironing
board…
so there is no return
and you might as well hang yourself
or jump from the precipice into the whirling waterfall!
One word can wound you so…
you just fall to the ground and
cry like a big puddle!

Love

I am shipwrecked upon that Wild Shore

You all know how bad it is for your health…
let alone
when you
ache
twitch
moisten
for

a younger man.

Well, there it slipped.
Out it's slipped.

I'm in love with a younger man.

A burst of loud, jolly, inappropriate music. She ignores it.

An actress of my generation is very easily injured
And no matter *how* famous she is for her sense of
    humour…
comments such as… 'hey, there's still steam in the old
boiler'…don't make me laugh a bit.
Not a bit.

Surely all the women of my generation,
ever since we were little girls…so little that it really

makes me
Cry, have been waiting and dreaming of love…
Where is it?
What is it like?
and when they've merely heard…just heard…that there's
somebody in love…or they've been in love…
they've actually
vibrated sort of…
at so holy
for a woman so total…
of both spiritual and bodily…
of life and death…
so frightening and inconceivable that it includes
everything
everything everything
without exception!
Everything!
And at the same time it's more important than any
other thing
in the world, more important than air or food, or sleep…
It Is!
Ever since you were a little girl…
life means waiting for love
just to get a glimpse of it…
or to be able only to watch others' happiness
from the corner of the eye…
or to admire it from afar and to shed tears…
Oh, at least to have some of That Sort of Thing going
on!!!
That's *Life*!
That's *Living*!

And then…
at My Age…
as a woman and an actress…
to realise that this fully self-sacrificing love of a woman
is being *manipulated*
Being used by *two* vain madams who have
A driving *need* to be in the Limelight! I'm not one
to tell tales but look in your programmes under
Writer!

look under
Director!

She encourages the audience to look in their programmes...names are named...

Well, I suppose the Main Point of this nonsense was to
create Advance Publicity for the Play!
Bums on Seats!
And Yet, *strangely* enough...although I... *I*...have left
The Show...*nobody* knows about it!!!
Nobody's Nipped off to the Newspapers about That!
They call me in, say, we've got an *extraordinary* play
from
Finland...
it's about *theatre*
and *art* and *philosophy*
and the existential *loneliness* of the human being...
but most of all it's about the power of love to redeem us
and we want you to be the female lead!

I read the first draft...
I said 'It's very Finnish. Very Lapp. Very
Scandinavian.'

The Adapter said
'I'm going to adapt all that.'

The Director said 'We think, with a few adjustments...
it could be very British-friendly
and we might get a British Council Tour of India'

I said 'Philosophy isn't exactly *sexy* in Great Britain'
and the Adaptor woman
said '*Absolutely*...I *love* intelligent actors...
we're going to find an archetypal stereotype that's more
typical of *our* societal infra-structure'
'Trust us,' said La Director.
The Translator... *Translator*...
don't make me *laugh*...
the only Finnish she can translate is *Finn Air*!...
and The Director...*please*...
couldn't direct *traffic*...
decide to 'use it'

my real life anguished love…
decide to 'incorporate it into the fabric of the play'
decide we can 'sell the show media-wise on the old bag
falling for a toyboy Love-Wrangle-Angle'!
So The Adaptor goes off and
Freely adapts…

I keep getting Drafts *toasty* from
the photo-copier…

My agent says 'Do it Darling.
No bloody Money but, I'm thinking Street Cred.'

First Day of Rehearsal.
The Director says
'Well, we've had a little read-through,
let's try it out on the floor
throw it about a bit
and then have a little chat…'

and I'm so professional…
I'm blind to what's going on…
so I actually enter into the *interminable*
discussions about *What Love Is*

we don't have rehearsals
we have debates
Group Therapy

*A large swan moves regally from one side of the stage to the
other… She ignores this…*

This Lot
The *Creative Team*
have no idea what it is to be
on stage playing a woman falling in love
with a younger man…
who *really* falls in love with the younger man
who's *playing* the younger man
so that she spends all her evenings nights coffee breaks
in private, one-sided conversations with him…
…with that beloved…*young*…man…
about
say

age…
which do you prefer…a *bud* or a full-blown rose?'
'a *cub*…or a *lioness*?'…

The stage is suddenly suffused with rosy light…

An experienced woman is a philosopher…she's…
Full of Ideas!
Men can't get that from these young girls!
No!

She starts to hyper-ventilate…

I'm losing my…
I'm…
I start to see such hazy dreams…pearly colours…

She does.

and my breathing…I can't control it at all…

She cannot…

an actress is always on the *verge* of expressing clear
images so that you believe in what you see…

She believes…

you are already feeling what you are saying…
you are already in the midst of that…
really…a whirlpool…

She is…

you know it pulls and tears and smashes…
and you can do nothing…
And the arteries are just ripping with the throbbing
of the pulse all over me!
In every bloody artery!
For God's sake! Look at Me!
My breathing stops!

*It does…for quite some time. The STAGE MANAGER comes out.
Looks at her. Is she dead? Stage smoke fills the space…after a
time… She is back. Breathing. Not acting. Exit SM.*

…I have to be honest

one reason for my departure was *indubitably*
the fact that the *Team*
all through rehearsal was only
interested in the *young* female character,

The lights grow slowly green… the LIGHTING DESIGNER is
clearly trying to pick up no-longer-played cues…

the one who plays my daughter…
or my daughter-in-law or something…
the writing's all very complicated…
she needed to be *advised*…and *shown how*…
and *whispered confidentially*
to…
and to me it's
'She's just to capture the *Youth* Demographic!'
I mean…it's all *'You* are…
The Name! The Talent! The Beauty!'
but then, behind my beautiful back, Lady Director's
ridiculing me to this young and completely
inexperienced actress…
because…she's *Young!*

Youth is Box Office!

You know the thing that I find *really* suspicious?
This young man…
With whom I will fall in love…
In *Finland*…the man who plays the

Finnish anthem starts loudly, then abruptly cuts out…

young professor of philosophy is played
by the *actual* young professor of philosophy!
He's twenty-one and he's a *star* in Helsinki!
The Finns watch him on TV.
They *listen* to what he says!
That's this Production's *Big Artistic Vision!*
…it really makes a mature woman laugh!
That's her *Directorial Thrust!*
Import from the *Finns!*

Oh yes…oh yes!

His name is *Himanen.*

A cherub flies across stage…

The next move is…
They suggest I play Himanen's *mother*!
If you want *Love* from me on stage…
Why make me *The Mother*?
And of someone I'm *actually* in love with!
They want to present a version of Oedipus Rex
The Adaptor's Sophocles
with '*Un Hommage*' to Hamlet…with me and
this girl doing the Gertrude/Ophelia thing…
and it's going to be very incestuous, but *Archetypal*…
with this Himanen as an Uber-Hero…
and *Me* as Uber-Mother…like I can't see through
the intellectualizing hogwash to 'You're a Bit Long
In The Tooth to Play the Love Interest!'
…and my elderly male colleague
who I haven't mentioned yet…is going to play either
Claudius or the father of Oedipus! …we get this Big
Lecture about 'The Uber-History of Western Theatre…'
Followed by her Idea…which is nothing more or less
than a *fricassee* of Shakespeare, Sophocles, and Chekhov
half-baked together into a lukewarm stew
of everyone else's ideas but with *her* as
Author
and Me as
The Mother!

I didn't know whether to laugh or cry!

*During the following passage, curtains twitch and eyes and faces
look out from backstage towards ELSA.*

Aha…
Look!
Some people lurking back there
my dear colleagues…
who snatched from me…
the rock upon which theatre is built…

She shouts to them.

An Actor's Confidence In Her Role!
Listen…

after I walked…
they got *Julie Goodyear* in to replace me!
As long as it's been in a *Soap*…
we were at Oldham Coliseum together!
Julie!
Can you hear me?

I know she's listening!

Good luck tonight, darling!
(*To audience.*) It is not my intention to delay and harm
the performance…
it's just that my heart is so full!
my professional pride so wounded
I've devoted my life to…this…
since I was a young, young girl…
it just makes me cry!

A play is a sort of…*joust*…of parts!

Mrs. Director actually *ripped* my part
out of my hands…a part she had written
for me …One she said she needed me for
…as a *name*…she said…it'll be *provocative*…
she said .. it's so *important*…she said…well, face it…
so necessary so provocative so important that I've
lost my job because of it!

This part of Himanen's mother…
gets cut…
not for the reason Mrs. Director is putting about…
that I refused to do love scenes with
my own son…
why…I don't mind…good heavens…we're
sophisticated people…it's in everyone's subconscious…
I've done Cutting Edge I've played Experimental!
Why…it was Sophocles himself who said
'In a dream everybody has lain with his mother'
in the new translation it even says 'fucked his mother'
If anything, this is liberating!
…no the reason it's been cut is

Scaredy-Cat Mrs. Director worried about audience
    reaction!
The Press Reaction!
Might slice into her royalties!
Money-grubbing, stingy, petty nobody!

Then she comes up with a version where
I'm a sort of Margaret Thatcher-type political
leader who is so in love with her son she
helps him get pecuniary Arms-Deals...
as if such a thing would happen!...
to finance his philosophy research...

Then a version where I'm the Queen...
and I give my son *Wales* as a present!...I *mean*...

Then there's a rewrite where I'm a
New Labour woman MP and I send my
son to a *public school*...I mean this woman
is so out of touch with real life...

and meanwhile
all the time
as actors we are improvising
around the idea of love...
that like the *trouper* I am
I took it on board so completely
that it just keeps surfacing...
so hot
so absolutely *crazy* as I've got about
Himanen...
Himanen...
philosophy...
that I get crazily-enthused and say...
let's take this *Cutting-Edge* Piece to Edinburgh next
year...
And next year's Edinburgh Theatre Festival
will be The Edinburgh Philosophy Festival!
Imagine...
Two drunks in The Festival Club...
'Is this can of special brew half full or half empty?'
Himanen keeps talking and I get so mixed up
that I start to promise him simply anything...

as long as I'm allowed to adopt him…
as long as I'm allowed to *have* him!

But why did I walk out

Well
this session we did
bare rehearsal room
me here
Himanen here
Mrs. Director there
I
I declared myself so profoundly…
so intensely….
like something out of a Russian novel…

She does so…

'I love you'… I said

The scene is so true, it gets the correct lighting cue…and music…

the actress to the philosopher
'I love you'
so real
so true
that it
that it
that it
frightened the shit out of Mrs. Director
and she cut it!
Why?
She is afraid of
I 'wasn't doing it right'…

She is terribly hurt…

and I was listening to her with head inclined
like that oh yeah…
And then I realise
She just wants to exploit me!
'Woman to woman'
Women let you down. They do.

Some very sad music plays. She looks at herself…

Why am I wearing this nightie?

What's that about, then?

Humiliation!

Over there I have a set of ecru underwear
hanging in a bag on a rack!

To wear in 'the savagely-revealing denouement'!

I'm a crazy, unbelievable character concept in the
work of a mean-spirited madam.

And when it dawned on me… I left!

There are better people to work with…
this lovely young Himanen for example…

We could both go to Finland.

I burned their script…
in my oil-fired Aga…

Snow falls…

very Hedda Gabler…
and thought…
you're now an actress without a role but…
improvisation is the child of stage-writing…
have a child
give birth yourself to a piece of work…

and here it is

something I worked on alone

a rough sketch of a part for an older woman…

She starts scene-setting…

I'm the female editor-in-chief
of a major newspaper…say *The Times*!
a sort of Rosie Boycott
and one day into my high-up office with its
huge windows and magnificent view
walks this young philosophy professor
from Finland

and he knocks me sideways
I'm *barkingly* madly in love with him
and his adorable ideas…
so much so, that every page of my newspaper
through my influence…
is *thick* with him and his ideas!
The Management gets wind of this…
'Editor Turns Broadsheet Into Love Rag'
and now… I'm being prematurely
pensioned off in order to maintain the face,
prestige and credibility of the newspaper!

She mentally, physically prepares…

As my last, courageous, idiosyncratic action
I decide to summon the editors and the
shareholders and the governing bodies here
to the Soho Theatre, Soho
which I have rented to
introduce Himanen to them!
And I'm saying…

She is in a strongly dramatic moment in a great classical play…

I have summoned you here tonight onto
neutral territory, owners and makers of
this great newspaper to ask you…
What is My Crime?

An ASM comes on a bit…starts searching through her script for this speech…as…

I have run the newspaper as I saw fit.
I report the news as I see the news
and the Big News for me is Love!
I give it a European Bias it's true…
I neglect American stories… I'm sorry…
but the Main Story *is* for *me* from *Finland*!
Too many column inches on 'Age Difference.
Does It Matter?' instead of fighting in Kosovo
in The Gulf, in Rwanda in Tamil Nadu?
Yes, yes, yes…
because for once, the news is *good*…
My whole editorial thrust *is* amatorial rather

than economical or political or despairing or...
What are your *precise* objections?
The size of his photographs on Page Three?
Were they too *big*?
Too *many*?
You think I *shouldn't* have printed the one
of his penis?
Women read newspapers *too*!
Remember *Diana*?
Yes...I filled the pages with tributes and
memories and people who knew him
because I wanted the streets to be
full of flowers!
The whole world *weeping*!
All hearts beating as *one*!
All this I've done because I *love*!
And I say it here
before *God*
...if that's a crime...
then *love* is a crime!
And now
I'll ask Himanen
to come in and talk to you
Himanen, come in!

ASM sidles off...

Even this welcome makes me...(*Faint with desire.*)
I...

HIMANEN has entered as if from the street. He is wearing outdoor clothing.

ELSA: There!
For God's sake! The adorable Finn! The Real Thing!

She goes to sit back in the audience...

Where shall I sit?
I can't see a thing!

Scene 2

HIMANEN sets down his briefcase and takes off his coat. He steps behind the lectern and begins his introduction. He is very sincere, academic, Finnish, sweet and young. He is not acting either...

HIMANEN: There's a notion
  to the effect that truly *provocative*
  Theatre is impossible
  these days.
  As I walked here from the tube station...
  I grasped in an instant what I need to speak about here!
  And I have a feeling that this visit will change my life!

ELSA: What a minute, wait a *minute*...
  This has been changed!
  This is a New Scene!

Throughout this scene, he will politely try to continue his thesis without being rude to her or include her...a boy bringing a strawberry to his mother...

HIMANEN: Not so very long ago...
  The Art World *provoked*!
  Great Art used to Violate Good Taste!
  It used to get A Reaction from An Audience!
  Now it is impossible.
  No one takes Offence At Anything!
  No one is Hurt any more by Art...
  It doesn't make people Angry enough!

ELSA: Oh, he gets right to it
  like a Viking axe splitting our
  Saxon skulls!

HIMANEN: I don't believe people have got lazier
  about getting furious...
  about *hating*...and expressing that hatred...
  Look at how we *hate* refugees...and express
  our hatred of them with Molotov cocktails!

  Indeed, people are spitting threats and
  shouting slogans louder than ever...
  everyone has a Big Loud Angry Opinion

which he writes in a newspaper or on a wall
or on somebody's head with a baseball bat!

ELSA: Keep it about *Art*...Darling...*Theatre*...
...we *know* they are
beating people in the dark *minutes* away
from here...and
shit posted through letter boxes
but get back to Art!

HIMANEN: There is no longer a consistent system
of moral values in society.
There was once...and it informed everybody...
even those who were violating it!
Now, it's gone.
Nobody knows how to behave.
And you know why?
Look at your city...
As I walked here I looked at the way
the buildings here are built and placed
church commerce and government
interfacing with one another...
I realise how impregnated you are with
middle class values...

ELSA: Bear with him...he's *terribly* Scandinavian...

HIMANEN: All your values and morality
were created by the middle class...
your right to education
your equality of opportunity...
the middle class wrested from the aristocracy...
with their equality and education they
created the middle class family...
built bookshelves for its books...
took it on theatre trips to see, on stage
their lives,
their values
themselves.
They saw, reflected there, their philosophy...
that an individual
has an innate right to rise, by his own devices
to the top.

But today, this philosophy is untenable
both in art and in life…
because the middle class,
as a force for change…
is dead.

ELSA: What?
I must be mishearing!
What?

She screams.

Middle Class *dead?*
You have the nerve to come from *Finland*
and tell us
that the middle class here are dead?
They're not dead, Darling, they're everywhere!
Look here at this bunch…
the place is *stiff* with them…

HIMANEN: But even if there are *individual* middle class
as an entire social class they are dead!

ELSA: They're not dead, Darling,
they're New Labour!
Hey…it may be true in Helsinki
but listen…the last place
on earth where they die…will be here!
We *are* Class!
Look at your sweet face…

HIMANEN: And if it is dead
which I believe it is
for we are all now in Europe deemed equal
we are now all without anything *ahead* of us
whose barricades we can storm…
everything to fight against is
behind us…
within us
in very truth *us*
we are thus fighting against *ourselves*
we are angry with *ourselves*
therefore *we* get angry
nobody out there gets angry with our

culture…one of the elements of which,
but a decoratively-central one…is
art…is theatre, where provocation
is an invention originating with the bourgeois
class values…*The Marriage of Figaro* set The
French Revolution in motion…although there
Were some other elements involved.

ELSA: Oh…this is Stirring Stuff!
If the show had been like this…I wouldn't
have walked out!
Yes…Yes!…I would have sat out the whole
play and watched this *marvellous* young man!
It has the depth and vision of
The Sermon On The Mount!
Men *do* know how to *talk*, don't they?
God…he's like *Jesus*!…

A burning cross blazes, as a rail of ecru underwear is taken from Stage Right to Left…

HIMANEN: So, our theatre doesn't provoke anyone to
anger, to outrage, to rushing in with burning
torches and igniting the foul scenery
because its values and emotions
are attached to a social class that has gone…
We cannot *aspire* as such…
what is respected, what is hidden from
others, what is celebrated, what is tragic, what is
to be proud of, what is beautiful, what is repulsive,
what is wrong,…what is loved…what is true…
are all now in our gift…

ELSA: Did he say love?
Yes he did!
Oooh, I'm feeling quite *hot*!

HIMANEN: So we haven't the aspirations to want them.
We haven't the frustration of not having them
Or the anger at being denied them
We do not defenestrate
We do not storm
We do not rush to pull to pieces

the finely-clad bodies of those more
privileged than ourselves
for we are there
we are them.

ELSA: Oh, how he talks, how he knows his subject!

HIMANEN: *WE* are our own hated enemy!

The rail of ecru underwear, in its wrong place, is taken back...

ELSA: I don't understand a word he's saying
but something here
inside *shrieks...*
'He's right, he's so right!
...I feel so *hot!*

HIMANEN: The invisible moral centre of the world
which creates and keeps watch over our values...
has died, it's gone!
Governments lie.
Banks cheat.
Unions don't protect.
Insurance doesn't cover.
The whole world lacks a center...
Like the Vatican in its day...
Or the Kremlin in Soviet heydays!
Now everything all over the world depends
Only on the rate of the dollar!

ELSA: I want to lick him
the Finnish Choc Ice!
the Scandinavian Magnum!

HIMANEN: There is only one credible aristocracy
left in the world today...
and that is
philosophers
everyone else is below us
so
history teaches us that
vis-a-vis
revolution...
there is no other possibility than that

philosophy will die!
Soon, in the tumbrils
soon, beneath the guillotine…
philosophers!
Philosophy?
We must kill it!

ELSA: Kill it?
(*Terrified*….) Over my dead body!
I'm not philosophical…but I am…*deep*…
Philosophy will not die!
Do you see…you are making my life *longer*?
I'll die without you and your philosophy!
(*Whispers.*) You're making me younger…
look at me now…
do you see it?
If you'll only feel my pulse you could sense
something *enormous*…you create life, new life
in me!
You are like God!
Because you are the youngest sage in
the world…you make me so young…that
I feel like a little girl, a youthful girl!
Fully irresponsible!
Ready for anything!
Anything whatsoever!

HIMANEN: You don't realize…
just as the death of the middle class has
killed off provocative Theatre…
so it is with philosophy!
The only people we revere these days
are professional footballers!
And Television Presenters!
And Boy Bands!
And Lottery Winners!
The single yardstick which guarantees
man's importance is competition!
Nothing but competition!
Winning is the culture of today!
Winning is Life!
But philosophy isn't about winning!

ELSA: Why isn't it?
    You can't win?????
    You can!
    Make it about winning!
    You're the professor of philosophy…
    develop a *new* philosophy…
    Enter. Take part!
    Come First!
    Look Out For Number One!
    Get Ahead Of The Game!

HIMANEN: Look Out for Number One?

ELSA: Yes!

HIMANEN: Look Out for Number One….

A moment of great sudden philosophical discovery… STAGE
MANAGER, dressed as a Chinese Revolutionary, shows Brechtian
Placards…written in English, German, and Chinese…

HIMANEN: The old philosophy is dead
    the new one is born…
    the new kills the old…
    and *I* initiate it…
    …Thanks to you, to you…
    the new *today*, the *now* philosophy of
    'look out for number one!
    be a *winner*!…

ELSA: Yes! Go with it! Run with the idea!
    Invent! Improvise…
    Be the first in the world to hit on this idea…
    I love!

Great mounting excitement…

HIMANEN: I'm the first in the world to think of…
    right, because of you…good Lord…'To the
    one in love everything happens as if for the
    first time in the world! The one in love sees
    everything for the first time in the world!
    The one in love is always the first human
    being in the world! Who experiences…
    everything as the first human being for the first time!'

Goodness, gracious…listen to me…
To be in love may well be the purpose
of everything!

*A sense of amazing fireworks… light dawning… planets collid-
ing… Stage Management think they have heard the final cue…*

ELSA: Love is like a last blaze!

HIMANEN: The last blaze of philosophy's fire before
it dies out!
You handed it to me.
You were the one!
Being Woman…only as a woman in all
her motherhood may!
Love as the purpose of life, may be the
flame of philosophy, discovered for the
first time in the world…
and the last to have been put into practise
And by me!
Twenty-one when I set it on its feet!
The purpose of everything, love!

ELSA: Don't stop…
Go…into the starting blocks…
spin your balls…
go to Win!
Then you can watch your reflection in
the mirror of success!

HIMANEN: Reflections…Narcissism!
Common narcissism…
The first in the world I hit on common Narcissism.
Narcissism common to everyone and an
individual ecstasy eroticised together for the
whole community!
Common narcissisticality!
Yes… (*He starts thinking about this new idea…*) Yes!…
Yes… yes…Yes!!!!

ELSA: Fuck old philosophy!

HIMANEN: Yes…fuck it!
yes…
yes…

ELSA: He's so pretty and upsetting...I'm feeling
so hot, so hot!

HIMANEN: And educational life!
And the military life!

A military sound cue leaps in halfway through...boots marching...

An army of philosophers!
I was the first!
I hit on it because of you pointing me in
The right direction!
Frederick The Great the first philosopher-
commander in chief in the world!
In the whole world.
Just imagine...
the very first in the whole world!
I'll join your army and turn every soldier
into a philosopher!

A military tramping of many boots...

Your government is militarising the whole
country secretly anyway...
And look at *your* world...Show Business...
your plays are all about concealed violence...
movies always have to get military plotwise...
and spy thrillers...
nobody catches on...
but there's a big Military Hype going on...
a doctor of philosophy,
all the way from Finland...
as young as this,
attacks the army,
Now the outrageously-young
Professor Himanen
uncovers the secret militarism of this nation!
I'll join the army and collect evidence!
I'll rip the cataracts from the eyes of
my contemporaries!

He exits, with brief case.

A streetlamp, street back drop brought on…martial music…which changes to the accordion lament of 'Lili Marlene'…a woman alone, smoking under a streetlamp…

ELSA: He's joining the army!
  The army *wrenches* the man from
  the very *arms* of a woman!
  Oh, the pain in my heart!
  When the women are always losing their men
  To the army…
  that is such a manly way to win honour…
  and the woman's tears and pleas won't help
  there at all…
  it's to the soldiers that women always lose their men…
  I can almost see the eternal fight…
  Both the Mother and the Father always
  pulling their male child to themselves
  and at last the army takes care of its own!

All the above removed, as…

Scene 3

KATE CURRANT, a young actress, out of her mind, enters from backstage and makes her way to where ELSA is. KATE CURRANT is not acting either.

KATE: Well, you've done it now!
  Julie's gone crying out of the theatre!
  She was weeping over there…and then she
  fucked off!
  So, you've got to save this show!
  The young hero returns from his spell
  in the army…he's in anguish…you're speaking…
  …take it away!

ELSA: But I haven't rehearsed this!
  I don't know the cuts!
  You should have burst into tears then…
  nothing's like we blocked it…
  You're not even wearing the same costume!
  And what have you got in your mouth?

KATE: A lighter!
I always have something in my mouth.
It's something we found after you fucked off.
A sort of visual character note.
I'm like... *essence* of oral fixation!
But otherwise my character's just the same only different.

ELSA: (*To audience.*)...*then* we couldn't decide whether
she's my foster daughter or my daughter-in-law!

She absent-mindedly tidies and fixes KATE, mother to daughter...

Actually...it was sort of beautiful...
she was necessary in providing a subplot to
the main plot of my love for Himanen...
She was acting as if *she* was Himanen's
girlfriend...therefore she could stay with me.
I actually adopted her...as the chief editor of
the newspaper.. after I found her in the morning
in my study after the burglary and she was
sleeping it off in the front of the drinks
cupboard! The gang of burglars had left
her there, their lady accomplice, stoned and
pissed, and they'd taken her papers and
identity.
But I find she's like a daughter to me...
only she falls in love with Himanen...
just like me! I, of course, am *deeply* jealous...
It's quite... *textured...*

KATE: The Adaptor got cold feet about the
newspaper office scene...so you found me
after the burglary here at your home, but
otherwise I'm playing it the same
only that I don't really
love anybody, I just open my legs for everybody!
I'm like essence of disaffected youth!

She is very cheery about this...

Look, they're coming on...
fucking help me...
I can't technically get there any more..
I'll just do it sitting down! (*She sits.*)

Wing It!
You got the experience… (*Name of ELSA.*)
Just for me!

*HIMANEN and THE SERGEANT-MAJOR enter through the
outside door with their luggage. Both of them are muddy and tired.
They are dressed in army fatigues. At first they look in vain for
ELSA'S understudy JULIE. Then they speak, in desperation, to
ELSA across the auditorium.*

HIMANEN: I can't speak…
I won't make it without the Sergeant-Major…
(*Breaks down in tears.*)
I can't manage without him.
He'll speak for me.

He wanders aimlessly about the stage, terrified and disorientated.

KATE: (*To ELSA.*) Answer him! Anything!
Do a riff on 'my boy back from a cruel war…'
Look at the state of him!
Male Brutality!
You got to save him!

*HIMANEN is being physically threatened all the time by THE
SERGEANT-MAJOR.*

ELSA: Heavens, what's wrong with him?
I can see the state of…but I've no role!
I'm not in your play any more!
Why don't you play it?
I'm just watching now!
I'm just audience!

SERGEANT-MAJOR beats HIMANEN…

No! I can't just watch…
Look…I'll come and stand up on stage!
But I won't act!
And I'm not coming back!

*ELSA goes onto the stage, but she will not act. The SERGEANT-
MAJOR speaks always as if he were a large, windswept parade-
ground. He is not acting because he has no idea he is in a play…*

SERGEANT-MAJOR: It's been agreed that I talk.
    It's turned out that The Finn has got
    compassionate leave
    from military service for the time being…
    because he couldn't *stick* it…
    he was scared of *shouting*!
    He's been sent back to grow up a bit
    and after a couple of years there'll be a review.
    But no call for pessimism, despite the state of him!
    He is out of shape and he's lost his spark.
    The whole problem in a nutshell is;
    Women deprive a weak man of his nature!
    I made it my job to make a man out of this
    chap…that's why he can't manage without me!
    He's become a little bit too quiet…
    but that's progress…
    a man mustn't be a chatterbox…
    and neither I am…
    although I have to be the chatterer here!

He continues to threaten and beat HIMANEN…

    But we've agreed on…and even roughly rehearsed
    this speech.
    When I noticed from the orderly's log…
    …that this chap did nothing
    but stalk the corridors sleeplessly
    all night long,
    I took him to sleep with me in my bed,
    to calm him down.
    I chattered humorously to him…
    I noticed that he's completely lost his sense
    of humour….and a sense of humour
    is imperative for a man, along with
    pubic hair…I mean, if
    there's no sense of humour emerging once there's
    a full growth of pubic hair…you have to step in
    there with a heavy hand!
    So, since your straight white chap usually has
    the best sense of humour…I started there in
    bed at night, to tell him Jim Davidson type
    jokes, Tarbuck, Bygraves, that sort of thing…

as well as straightening out stuff from his
civilian circumstances!
Because I know about *you*, Lady!
I've got a fairly clear picture of
what's been going on between the two of you…
you can call it '*philosophical debate*' if you like!
I know you've tried to get him a job on
your newspaper as philosophy correspondent
and he's ready to take that on
…once he has become less…silent
and framed up and opened his mouth and
spun us a yarn.
I've bought a laptop from a computer warehouse
Soon I'll start getting the lad used to it.
First I'll dictate and he'll write…
then he just might start producing philosophy!
I take full responsibility for the last blaze
in the death of philosophy…
that's one project…
and also for the vaster project of making a
man out of him…
so that he can measure up to his mission.
But I want us to run a tight ship
spit-and-polish, Queen's regulations
nothing too civilian
nothing too sloppy…!
I can't work with that!
It would be easier to just grab you by the throat!
I'm slightly out of control.
Damn it, listen Himanen!
It is no joke, no joke, Himanen, so
help you God!
It's no joke!
Better believe it once and for all, Himanen!
Without further ado, Himanen!
Do we agree?
(*HIMANEN nods.*)
Well, now we can carry on fixing the future,
the future for us all!
Okay, I've made an agreement with Himanen,
verbally…

and shake hands on it (*He does.*)…as between
man and man…
and I'm used to counting on verbal agreements
so that's binding…and I understand that
Himanen's got a remunerative deal from you…
so you should know that I have been hired
as Himanen's personal security consultant
and fitness trainer and
educator of his willpower.
Let's call a spade a spade…I am making a
man out of this chap!

KATE: Don't they have *long* speeches in Finnish Drama?
Apparently, over there…the populace like
really wants to see stuff…so you can just
write…(*Mime for on and on and on…*)

SERGEANT-MAJOR: My salary is a thousand a month
with full bed and board.
I don't need days off…
nor holidays.
I'll be keeping on at Himanen day and night
all year round.
Shall we shake on it?

ELSA: A thousand a month?
There'll be nothing left out of my savings for
living!
A thousand a month?

SERGEANT-MAJOR: Plus bed and board.

ELSA: Who do you think you are?

SERGEANT-MAJOR: I am sergeant-major Tommy
Thompson,
fifth light infantry…from which battalion
I've gone AWOL, because there's been no
time to apply for leave because of the
Himanen Death of Philosophy
Emergency Situation!!
I gave a command that we walk in full marching
kit from Aldershot…
but by Woking this Himanen chap is so knackered…

I couldn't carry him across my shoulders
on account of having *two* packs in my
hands so we took the train from Woking…
but we marched as far as Woking,
though not in step all the time…
and I didn't demand a crying man should
keep in step…
except of course when we
passed through built-up
areas!
Still, that's progress
Aldershot to Woking!
Immediately you see the self-esteem rise…
no matter how big a snivelling weakling he is!
When I see that…
I forget the pain of the journey!
The kicking, the beating, the threats!
If he is a rag *now*…
then he was something you could
wipe up with a rag!
He'll sleep now!

ELSA: A thousand a month?
To you? On a newspaper editor's salary?
There'll be nothing left out of my savings!
How on earth can we make ends meet?
Three people!

SERGEANT-MAJOR: Plus bed and board!

ELSA: And where do you think you'd be living?

SERGEANT-MAJOR: With Himanen.
Same room same bed.
And between you and me…keep your
voice down…as soon as you threaten him
with sleeping alone he gets upset.

ELSA: What?
I support you…and you sleep every night
together with Doctor Himanen?
Sharing a bed?
What?

In the same bed?
(*To HIMANEN.*) Dear one
What have they Done To You?…
I was crazy to let them let you join the army!
I have here with me a young, young foster daughter.
I'll make you fall in love and then you
needn't go off looking for love…
(*To KATE CURRANT.*) Present yourself.

KATE: (*Something in her mouth obscures her speech.*)
I am Kate Currant.

SERGEANT-MAJOR: What?

KATE: Currant. Blackcurrant, you make blackcurrant juice
out of it for flu. I'm like, a cure, for
society's malaise, yeah? God!

SERGEANT-MAJOR: I just want to make it clear
in my presence, there must be no criticism
of God. I have sworn a soldier's oath… 'So help
me God'…and I can't take a joke about it…or
follow a philosophy which doubts the holy book!

KATE: Sorry! (*She's not.*)
Can't say 'God' now…

Burning cross effect appears…

SERGEANT-MAJOR: I tell you pointblank, the lad's misery
is mostly due to this…
His head had been stuffed with *doubt*!
Doubt makes you sick… so with me no
doubts, no non-patriotic behaviour, no humanitarianism,
and especially no whores…
is that clear?
Whores?…over my dead body!
I'm keeping guard on him here!
Whores are something I can smell from afar…

KATE: I'd like you to give me a military education!

SERGEANT-MAJOR: What?
That…that…that God damned thing was why
I fled from the army!

ELSA: (*To KATE.*) What have you got in your mouth?

KATE drops a thick, gold man's necklace from her mouth.

KATE: This. It's male jewellery.

ELSA: Whose male jewellery? Where did you get it from?

KATE: I found it.

ELSA: Found it? Where?

KATE: The street.
I ingest street wisdom.
I've got two spellings of my name, yeah...
c u r r a n t...and c u r r e n t...

Puts the necklet in her bra and takes out some coins and puts them in her mouth.

I suppose it means I'm like...
current...I'm like...a metaphor...for *now* values...yeah?
And I subtext-wise...embody the consumer ethos...

ELSA: (*Notices that KATE has her panties in her hand, which she throws aside...*) Have you got knickers on?

KATE: S'nobody's business what I have under my skirt!
I don't have to answer, yeah?
Course I'm wearing knickers.

ELSA: So what are these then? Scotch mist?
Turn round. (*She checks.*)
Good Lord!
Why no knickers?

KATE: I started to feel so hot.

SERGEANT-MAJOR: I won't intervene in this!
...My position on this is known!

KATE: Oh right, is it? (*To HIMANEN.*) This him? (*Shakes hands.*)

She is strongly physically affected by HIMANEN...

What is his hand doing to me...bringing to my mind...
what can the feel of his hand recall...?

ELSA: This is where she falls in love with him?
This won't work…

But she is too philosophically moribund to sustain it…

KATE: Sod it…he's not doing anything for me…
I'm morally moribund…
I'll go cadge some cigarettes…

ELSA: Are you going to the bar?

KATE: Well, you can't smoke in here.
And why should I pay for them when I can
cadge them? (*Exits.*)

ELSA: (*Notices the panties, grabs them.*) Well put your knickers on!
Not going anywhere with no knickers!

KATE: I'm so hot.
It's just so tiring wearing knickers
when you're bumming fags!

ELSA: You'd rather walk round with them in your hand…
so everybody knows you've got nothing under
your skirt but hair!

KATE: Well, okay…I'll put them on as soon as you close
the door!

ELSA: I want to see that you put them on!

KATE: Well, I'll come in there to put them on then!

ELSA: No you don't!
You can put them on there…
I'll close the door.

SERGEANT-MAJOR: It's alright with us, if you want to
put your knickers
on inside, isn't it, Himanen?
It doesn't affect us in any way,
does it, Himanen?

HIMANEN: No…

ELSA: Change here…quickly!

KATE: (*Putting on her panties.*) I don't really get it...
why can't you give me a military education..?

SERGEANT-MAJOR: It's a male thing...
Don't get me started...
you....

KATE exits.

ELSA: If you as much as once mention 'whore', you'll
have to leave!

HIMANEN: Oh don't...

ELSA: What! Can't I get rid of him?

HIMANEN falls to the floor with fatigue and grief.

HIMANEN: Tomorrow my life will be devastation!

ELSA: What did you say?
Why will your life...

HIMANEN: Tomorrow will be too late...

ELSA: Now, now, isn't it better for this man to leave
so we can talk...? Tell him to go...Why, you don't talk
freely when he is...
Why, you don't say anything...

She starts to cry when she sees that HIMANEN is fast asleep...

SERGEANT-MAJOR: Thank your lucky stars he fell asleep!
Shame on you, you old woman!
You have no understanding of a man's soul!
You know nothing about manliness and the might
of man!
You treat me like a nobody!
And its starting to get on my nerves!
And though you pretend to have a relationship
with this boy...
you just let him lie there asleep!
You pretend woman and man stuff is involved...
but you don't let him go to bed!

ELSA: What do you know about us?

The SERGEANT-MAJOR starts to unpack his bags.

SERGEANT-MAJOR: Over there…a *warrior* is sleeping…
and there's *no* bed in sight!

ELSA: And there won't be a bed…until you tell me
what you've heard about him and me!

SERGEANT-MAJOR: I know what kind of man you want
to make him into!
Well, watch out!
I've read books *too*!
I've written out stuff *in long hand*!
fat books! *Big Words*! *Finnish Writers*!
Vaino Linna!!!!! for one! And…*Vainno Linna*!!!!
Now I've retired from the army…
I'll have a lot of time for reading
so… just watch it.
Now, if it's alright with you, I'm going to
fasten a climbing rope to the ceiling
so that in the night,
I can send the lad up it
…if he gets scared in a strange place.

He takes out hanging ropes. We are in the valley of the shadow of death…

SERGEANT-MAJOR: Here we are!
I am a man of profound…ness.
I've always lived in the shadow of death.
Death and love…they belong together.
You, as a woman, may have visited the place
of love more often…but death is my companion,
my closest companion…my best friend, really!
Geddit?
For years and years I have made it my hobby
to collect hanging ropes.
The actual ropes of men who hang themselves, look.
Suicidal Aids, look.

The ropes hang here and there…

SERGEANT: I buy them from the relatives.
I've got some of them from gravediggers…

slip 'em a backhander…they get them for me
out of the coffin.

ELSA: People hung themselves with these?
Really?

Deathly music…a solitary violin…plays…

SERGEANT-MAJOR: In the noose of every one of
these…someone
perished!
First they struggled…
Then they dropped!

*Someone in Design had the good idea of making the Ropes signifi-
cant. Ropes are pulled out of the bag on very visible wires and the
head up into the roof like snakes up a tree… ELSA and THE
SERGEANT watch perplexed…*

There's nothing dreadful about death.
You just have to get close to it.
You'll survive the explosion if you
stand really close…further off, the guts blow up.
These have been of great help to Himanen,
haven't they, Himanen?
Himanen!

ELSA: Stop!

The music…reluctantly…stops…

You!
Assaulting a frail and sensitive young man!
You've taken him over and you're planning to
make money out of him
You are a monster…
you're a black hole…

SERGEANT-MAJOR: What are you talking about?
This is idealism!
I'm a married man!
And then a divorced one when she
went off with someone else!
I won't let Himanen be destroyed like that!
No whores!

ELSA: Get out of my sight!
   I can't look at you!

SERGEANT-MAJOR: Look at me!
   It's not just the whores!
   The whorishness of women!
   The whorishness of whorish women!
   It is the thing, whoredom itself!

ELSA: Let me go!
   I'll shout so loud that everybody'll come…

SERGEANT-MAJOR: He'll be a great man, if I keep him from
   Whores…and what they do!
   That's what wears a man down…
   the *fucking*!
   (*He makes terrible gestures…*)
   You women started it!
   I can't bear this free-for-all fucking!
   If I so much as hear a whisper in favour
   of fucking…
   Fucking women shall not gain a foothold,
   not one inch…
   Fucking women leap at your throat if you
   don't get a move on!
   It's merciless!
   And this chap is feeble in the face of fucking!
   I swear, he will not be destroyed by it!
   Is that clear, everybody?
   Don't you worry Himanen, don't panic!
   Rest in peace!
   If only there was a bed!
   We need a bed!

Stage hands try to carry a bed onto the stage…

ELSA: Do we really need a bed for this scene…?
   Oh, alright then, bring the bed on!

Stage-hands are manoeuvring a bed into the room. There are bedclothes on the bed.

ELSA: Oh no, I'm not supposed to make the bed, am I?

SERGEANT-MAJOR: I am an expert bedmaker, obviously,
  but I think that's a woman's job…
  so I'll help you undress Himanen…

ELSA: (*As she makes the bed…*) I know their plan!
  They are hoping I'll fall in love with
  this weird character! It won't happen!

SERGEANT-MAJOR: A bed made by a woman!
  Now, Himanen, here a man doesn't need
  to be ashamed of his emotions!

ELSA: Are they getting in there?
  Together? For God's sake!
  A doctor of philosophy and that…
  Goodness gracious what shall we do now?
  There they are!

SERGEANT-MAJOR: It's been such a difficult day…
  I get right down on my knees to say my
  goodnight prayers…

He says his prayers, kneeling, by the bed…

ELSA: There he is now with his head on my pillow,
  but my head is not on the same pillow.
  My head is alone!
  What did he say…that he will be 'devastated'…?
  'Tomorrow' was it?
  Will this marvellous genius creature of God's
  be destroyed?
  Do I have to wait till the other one has fallen asleep!
  maybe then he will have the courage to
  open up…open up to me…
  Oh, it hurts!…to see him like
  this…

SERGEANT-MAJOR: Has anyone anything to say before I
  nod off?
  No.
  Okay then…
  'Lights Out!'

The lights go out and the SERGEANT-MAJOR goes to sleep beside HIMANEN in the bed. ELSA sneaks into bed on the other side as...

(*Whispers.*)...even though it's Lights Out...
Do you want to hear any jokes?

HIMANEN: Oh no.

SERGEANT-MAJOR: That's it then.
Now, fall asleep through sheer strength of will!
Follow my example, Himanen...
It's such a long time since I slept in a
bed made by a woman.
Such a long... (*He starts to snore.*)

ELSA: That's it?
They 'both fall asleep?'

Lights start to fade...

But there's no *build*!
No plot twist to leave on!
You can't make this the...

Lights snap off...

Interval!!!!

Interval.

ACT TWO

Scene 1

The three of them are in bed. The SERGEANT-MAJOR is snoring gently. An ASM is caught out as the lights come on. Exits.

ELSA: (*Whispering.*) ...I can't sleep!
Not until you tell me what's happening tomorrow.

HIMANEN: No...

ELSA: Are you afraid of him...?

HIMANEN: No.

ELSA: Of me?

HIMANEN: No...

ELSA: What is it?
What's frightening you?
...this suffering...its unbearable!
What's happening?

HIMANEN: Tomorrow... (*He bursts into uncontrollable tears.*)

ELSA: What about tomorrow? What have you done?
Don't be afraid, I'll save you...
How can I help you?
I'll give you everything...

HIMANEN: No help...for me...there's...

ELSA: Why not? Something can always be done!
Where there's life there's hope!
You're alive!

HIMANEN: Tomorrow... I'm not...

ELSA: Who is coming tomorrow?
Is it someone frightening?

HIMANEN: …devastation…

ELSA: Something happens tomorrow? What?

HIMANEN: …tomorrow…twenty-two…

ELSA: Is it a bill? …twenty two thousand…twenty two
   million…twenty two debt collectors…?

HIMANEN: …twenty two years… I…it will all be over…

ELSA: Hang on a second…
   is it…
   is this…
   …Is it because tomorrow you will be twenty two????

HIMANEN: It is all over…Tomorrow!

ELSA: You're telling me? Me?
   You're whimpering that life is over…and you
   are a child! A child! What do I have before me?
   Tell me! Tell me!

HIMANEN: I'm…too old…tomorrow…

ELSA: Now my heart…my heart's *shattering*!
   Remember…you're the one who tore my
   heart to pieces.

HIMANEN: …before the morning of my twenty-second
   birthday…
   I must…kill myself…

ELSA: What? …you have a life ahead of you…
   what do I have?… (*She shakes him desperately.*)

*ASM steals back for her cigarettes, lighter, book and mobile
phone…*

HIMANEN: …a life thrown away…now over…death…

ELSA: It's cold…
   …feel my hands…
   my blood's turning to ice!
   (*She screams.*)
   Don't touch me!

The SERGEANT-MAJOR cries out in his sleep…

HIMANEN: Quickly…I have to…

ELSA: Don't leave me!

HIMANEN: (*Back in bed.*) Tommy, Tommy, what is it…

SERGEANT-MAJOR: (*Cries.*) Where am I… Anneka…
    Anneka, is it you…
    …Himanen, what the devil…

HIMANEN: You're shouting in your sleep…

SERGEANT-MAJOR: Where's the old woman
    …didn't hear, I hope…
    You're a philosopher… tell me…
    …How can a man asleep be so helpless?
    …in the night I'm like an old woman…
    I dreamt about my marriage… (*He cries.*)
    she took away my faith,
    and now…nothing
    at all…alone into the misery of old age…they
    pour hot coffee down your throat…and there's
    nothing a man can do…the woman nurses think
    of nothing but restaurants and dancing…nurses
    with giant tits…the only thing you can smell is cunt.
    Lipsticks the main interest…and phoning their
    boyfriends from the workplace…and there, the
    old man lying helplessly…hot coffee poured
    down the throat…and there's nothing the man
    can…if there are no relatives…who they are
    afraid of…swinging their asses, thinking of
    dance floors…taking away the man's meal…
    if he eats too slowly…and coffee hot into the
    throat…since I don't have any relatives…

HIMANEN: You have me…I'd come, only I commit
    suicide tomorrow…

SERGEANT-MAJOR: Now enough,
    enough…tomorrow's a hard day…

HIMANEN: (*Bursting into tears.*) I can't face tomorrow…
    twenty *two*, not *one*!

It will look totally different on a tombstone…
and in the biography…
Let me go…I am done…

SERGEANT-MAJOR: Stop feeling threatened!
If its out there, don't meet it with a tremble!
Only old women use that Old Trembling Trick!!

HIMANEN: I have caused her terrible…she is going to lose
her job because of me…

SERGEANT-MAJOR: They are nothing but women, they
ought to suffer.
Stop bawling! You can bawl in your sleep!
Just like me!
Women folk shed tears in each others arms.
And blackmail with 'I'll kill myself, I'll kill myself'
But at agony, at blood, they take flight!
There'll be a little bit of pain…but it'll give you back
your taste for life!
Trust me!

He hits HIMANEN.

ELSA: This is not what we rehearsed!
Please somebody…one of you men…pull
them apart!…we've no idea what
he might do!
(*To SERGEANT-MAJOR.*) I saw you hit Dr
Doctor Himanen, here in my flat…that's
unprovoked assault and there are plenty of
witnesses!

She goes to the stove…

I've got boiling water here…and since I am
legally entitled to defend
my old man against attack in my own home…

*An ASM, followed by dry ice, brings on a pan of water, puts it on
stove, exits…*

ELSA: I'm within my rights to turn you into a
steamed pudding!

There is a free-for-all… with the men fighting…and her shouting imprecations and threats all the time, until…

ELSA: Men!
Violence!
The martial tradition!

SERGEANT-MAJOR: Okay…if no one trusts my methods.
So long Himanen!
Good riddance to the man for whom I left
the army!

He packs his bags as…

HIMANEN: Look what you've done!
He's packing his bags!

ELSA: He can't hit you in front of Newspaper people!

SERGEANT-MAJOR: I'm not staying here to be insulted!

HIMANEN: He is leaving me!
Stop him!
He was the one who saved me and kept me alive!
Now I'm getting in a panic…I can't bear it…
I'm going to cry! Doooon't leeeeaaaaave…!
Doooon't leeeeeet gooooooooo!
I'll Stop speaking!
No more Philosophy!

ELSA: I do *everything*…
he calls for *him*!
You give them all the milk from your breast…
the first word they learn….*Daddy*!
(*She is suddenly horribly confused…*)
Is he my *son*?

HIMANEN: Aaagh….

He bites his tongue to remain silent and purses his lips as if he is eating them…

Help me, Tommy! I am swallowing
My Tongue!
I can hardly breathe!

He bites the bedclothes, the bedpost, anything...

SERGEANT-MAJOR: ...didn't I say he'd go apeshit?
    Just this once!

Comes up to HIMANEN, punches him in the stomach...
HIMANEN grabs him by the arm...

HIMANEN: I won't let go of this hand!
    I'll hang on to it until we join the foreign legion...

ELSA: Me, it's Me Here!

HIMANEN: There's nothing you can do about them!
    Those in the barrack room!
    respect nothing!
    Not intellect, not anything!
    The sergeant-major protected me!

ELSA: Try to control yourself!
    Maybe you should have a sauna...
    something *from Home* to calm you down...

HIMANEN: Charcoal fumes! They're taking me by force
    into *smoke*! You'll need four men to stop
    me beating my brains out on the walls and floor!
    I'm Panicking!
    The world isn't getting any better!

He struggles and rages by himself.

ELSA: One word...just listen to just one word!
    The future!
    Our future!
    Come here and let me massage your shoulders!

SERGEANT-MAJOR: He's gone apeshit...
    Massage won't work!
    He's going to be like this for hours!

HIMANEN: I can see faces!
    Not to the sauna...don't take me to the sauna!
    I won't talk...I won't talk!
    Sergeant-Major, Tommy, help me!

He starts to climb the rope...

Don't take the rope away…suffering will
make me a man!
Look! Here! I'm climbing!

SERGEANT-MAJOR: Oh, now's he's gone apeshit climbing!

ELSA: Come down…don't stay up there!…
Shall I come up?

HIMANEN: Don't you see…I'm already in a void!
(*He is stretching out his hands, meddling with the lighting rig.*)
I'll electrocute myself if the Sergeant-Major leaves!
I'll get an electric shock and Fry!

SERGEANT-MAJOR: We're lucky this isn't
a high pine forest…
as you might get in Finland…
otherwise he'd be swinging from branch to
branch! He's foaming at the mouth!

ELSA: Take the fuses out!

She rushes to the electricity meter at the rear of the stage. We hear a cry.

Fade out!
He'll get an electric shock!
I can't work these fuses out!

There is a full blackout. Lighting box, sound box, everything.

LIGHTING ENGINEER: (*S/O.*) Now the whole bloody
house is blacked out!
Don't touch anything.
It's short-circuited!
I'm coming down!

The LIGHTING ENGINEER heads for ELSA.

HIMANEN: Not in the Dark Forest!
Anything But The Dark Forest!

ELSA: This is Existential Angst!!!!
He's gone Strindbergian!

HIMANEN: I'm afraid of the forest!
Forest and Dark!

ELSA: Where are you?
  Listen, Sergeant-Major. If you're there,
  help me catch him!
  Doctor Himanen!
  Where are you?
  Dear one!
  Come out!
  Show yourself!

SERGEANT-MAJOR: He won't give himself up for hours!
  Okay…I'm making tracks!
  I'll leave the rope in the ceiling as a
  reminder of me…do you hear me,
  Himanen…wherever you are?

SERGEANT-MAJOR leaves.

HIMANEN: Doooooooon't!

ELSA: Got you!
  Stop wriggling! Gently now!
  Your heart is beating as fast as a baby rabbit's!

HIMANEN: But he's going… Light…give me light…

ELSA: Now stay still and calm down!
  Try to let your breathing pattern mine!

HIMANEN is panting madly…

ELSA: No, never mind, I'll try to catch up with you!
  This is how we breathe!

HIMANEN pants heavier…

  In the dark together, like this!

HIMANEN: Light!

ELSA: No, no light!
  We don't need any light now!

HIMANEN is going apeshit…

ELSA: This is us both calming down together!

The lights go on….

Oh my own beloved Jesus Christ!

HIMANEN: I'm frothing at the mouth!
Don't let them see…

ELSA: You're biting your lips…in the
dark I was so hoping to feel them on mine…

SERGEANT-MAJOR: (*Re-entering.*) …one of
my hanging ropes is missing!
Where is it, Himanen?

HIMANEN shows him the rope and looks penitent.

ELSA: Now I'm going to explode!
Here it comes!
I'm going to get it off my chest, from the
depth of my heart…
Look at him!
The most wonderful philosopher in the
world is eating, swallowing his own lips
because our miserable, unspiritual
'philosophy-what's-*that*?'
society won't let him speak!
You beat him up!
Look at me…I'm bursting into flames of
anger like a church struck by lightning!
My lips are crying holy, holy, holy!
And my organ pipes are belching flames,
burning hot resounding the hymn of Himanen
I'll equal the Army in Fire Power on this!
I'll out Sun the Sun in influence!
Be afraid…Be Very Afraid!
Loves Conquers All!

HIMANEN: Don't…let me go! I can't! No academic
told me it's A Man's World!
A dissertation is no better than toilet tissue!
I'm the most miserable M.Phil. in the whole world!

ELSA: Dear…see yourself,
alone, weeping, high up against the sky…
feeling the entire despair of a man of genius…
it's like being surrounded by a huge fire

raging, burning in the forest of your intellect…
but I am gathering like a huge rain cloud above
him…squatting on a hole within the
terrifying flames…and his agony
makes me swell, expand, moisten for the
protection of Him…turns me into a
huge, damp cloud and I am wet! Wet!
And I rain on him, and my moisture waters
the germs of ideas…and…
I feel you inventing things…
For our purpose here on earth is to be in love!
All social life is constructed round it!
Good Lord!
My dear own doctor Himanen here
is bombarding the atom…
is splitting the atom of love
and it's exploding…he's the Niels-Bohr of Love!
And I'm radio active with him!
His experiment shows me the meaning of
human existence!
I have to let the United Nations know what he
has discovered in me…
how they'll shower him with Peace Prizes…
He has Made Me Come!

She does…

Everybody from backstage pops their heads through to see…

HIMANEN: In the barracks they speak such smut, such
   smut
   and say such terrible things about women, say
   that there's no such thing as love…
   …I can't bear it…I can't bear it!

ELSA: Forget the army, forget it!
   Enlist in my unchained, natural, brutal, female
   bestiality…! …for God sake's,
   look at me, am I
   dancing…? I'm a runaway horse, a wild
   animal…there's a ringing in my head…
   my mind's in a daze!
   Touch me!

Don't put me on a pedestal!
Forget the Army! Join Me!

HIMANEN: No, I can't!
Life has tired me out!
Twenty-one vain and empty years!
Man is not made for such an ordeal…
to run such a gauntlet of miseries as these
twenty-one years have been!
Now I see my philosophical brilliance
was just a flash in the pan!
You who are coming after me…work hard
Study what she's saying…
(*He cries…*)
because I don't remember, I can't, I can't, I can't…

ELSA: Join me, join me in this, in my phantom runaway
train…I let my whistle blow and I fling sparks
from my pan to the dark woods of the world, the
birds fly up with fluttering feathers, singing
the intellectual superiority of Himanen!

HIMANEN: Down with science!
Down with intellect! Stupidity rules! Only
stupidity is good! Only out of stupidity can
something good arise!

ELSA: Inside here…I'm being carried away again…
am I deceiving myself? I can see you shouting…
but I hear something different…You only
need to shake your head and a hot wind
heads and eyes appear again…she's coming again…
engulfs me! And it whisks me into a whirlwind
and pulls me up root and branch like a tree from
the forest, up to strange heights…now I hear a
voice whispering for the first time ever…
'The huge memory preserved by the subconscious
is like a great archive to the conscious: what
has been seen or heard, can be remembered.'

This appears as backdrop, in large red text…

Consider what a human being will then be
capable of doing…

HIMANEN: Let me die…
  …you who still have a life before you…
  you want to get on…be an Idiot!

ELSA: I'm carried away…I'm an overflowing river
  boiling, breaking foaming rapids…

SERGEANT MAJOR: (*Waking, shouting.*) Under the water,
  whore!
  Drown the whore!
  Where am I? I dreamt I was drowning a whore…

HIMANEN: Tell me again about War…

SERGEANT-MAJOR: Ah, once…
  once upon a time officers were nobles…
  and the men…peasants…
  And the officers had swords and small arms
  and drove the men ahead of them…poking
  them with the swords and shooting them in the back
  And the noblemen brought up the rear,
  protected by the whole lot!
  But when *Democracy* came along,
  and *Equality* got the upper hand,
  then the officers got in front of the
  frontline, to lead those that come behind!
  Follow, God Damn!
  It sends cold shivers down!
  Does it send cold shivers down you?

Water pours and drips somewhere…

HIMANEN: Yeee… aaah… damn it…

SERGEANT-MAJOR: God damn!
  That's what War is all about!
  Us on behalf of the officers!
  And the officers on behalf of us!
  All for one and one for all!
  Just like the Three Musketeers! Les trois…
  What I like about France is the French brothel,
  which I have not visited,
  as opposed to the British brothel,
  which I have.

The French have riding whips, the
spurs, the opium pipes of local culture,
every possible contraption, white gloves
in their hands…looking high and low through
a monocle for whores…long cigarette
holders, damn it, which extend…you see,
sadists…with white gloves…they don't even
touch a woman with their bare hands because
they're too sophisticated, you know…that's
where I would've wanted to be!
Then my marriage too would've…
(*He bursts into tears.*)
I failed to do her in…

ELSA: Can you imagine the dreams I've had about us?

The SERGEANT-MAJOR jerks awake again, horrified, gulp with air at the horror of his dream…

SERGEANT-MAJOR: I had a terrible dream!
uuuughuuugh…I dreamt
that the gal, who was here, this…yours…the one
who left…and the panties…I dreamt that she was
my daughter…

KATE CURRANT enters excited and out of breath. She is dressed in a bikini made out of whipped cream, with nothing on underneath. On one wrist and one ankle she has a handcuff…with the other clasp undone. She is drunk and she has gentlemen's cufflinks and a glass eye in her mouth.

SERGEANT-MAJOR: Well, bumming cigarettes, were you?
Is somebody after you?
Why are you so breathless?

KATE: I'm not breathless, I'm excited!

ELSA: What? Handcuffs? Where are your knickers?
Where are your clothes?

SERGEANT-MAJOR: Please tell us, that you have them on
underneath all…
That…

KATE: This is whipped cream swimwear! I've come to show
  myself to Himanen and get licked by everybody!
  I'm like… essence of consumable!

SERGEANT-MAJOR: That's what is it! Whipped cream!
  Right down to her
  pubic hair!

ELSA: To show Himanen! Like a layer cake! And licked?
  What have you got in your mouth now?
  Don't show me… I'll have to leave!

SERGEANT-MAJOR: Gold and whipped cream!

*KATE drops elegant cufflinks, rings and a glass eye from her
mouth…*

KATE: Of course it's whipped cream!
  The subtextual message is that
  only by licking a woman's body can you find out
  what she's really like!

SERGEANT-MAJOR: These are pure gold…with
  monograms on them…
  and…hell…whose glass eye is this, I wonder?
  And wedding rings! Old ones! BC…Bill
  Clinton…and…TB…Tony Blair!

KATE: I snatched them when they pawed me…!

ELSA: Be quiet! For heaven's sake! I know this eye…
  it's David Blunkett's!

KATE: I snatched it while he stared and stared at me…!

ELSA: I'll get it back to his wife!
  I've had dinner with them…

HIMANEN: Do we…do we have to…to lick her?
  We have here…a philosophical metaphor made flesh!

ELSA: Handcuffs! You, you, where from? Quickly…
  where are they from?

KATE: Well, I don't know! The only possibility I can
  think of is, while they were whipping this cream…

one gentlemen threw his dinner jacket round my
shoulders...and in the sleeves...
were the handcuffs!
And they've been there ever since...and I've not
even noticed them!

SERGEANT-MAJOR: She could be telling the
truth...nowadays...
politicians...

ELSA: Politicians! At that sort of party! I suppose it
says so in your script! Attack New Labour!
Now I'm getting out of this play!
I'm not performing with naked creamed-up slappers!
The symbolism is completely out of hand!
you can inform the gutter press...
'Provocative Theatre?'
I was provoked right off the stage and out
of the auditorium!

SERGEANT-MAJOR: No, stay!

KATE: Let me lick your fingers clean!

She cuffs HIMANEN to her and begins to carry him off...

I'll take Himanen somewhere and rehearse him
until he's performance pitch...

ELSA: Take someone from the audience...
Himanen...don't go with her!

HIMANEN: (*Licking cream from both pairs of hands.*)
You know, the middle class has
elevated even decadence into culture!
Do you know that you bear
quite a remarkable resemblance to
turn-of-the-century pornographic material!

ELSA: No! No!

*She continues to shout and struggle under the SERGEANT-
MAJOR's lines.*

SERGEANT-MAJOR: We'll show you pornographers
suitable for all practicalities! We can do sadism without
philosophy! No need for riding whips here!

ELSA: You two over there! Himanen!
(*To SM.*) You let them go by themselves!

SERGEANT-MAJOR: I'm keeping you under my control!
Calm down now, woman! Or I'll put you over my knee!

ELSA: Don't try it! I'm in such an uncertain temper!
I won't be quiet! You started this with your
disturbed dreams!
How could he do this to me?

SERGEANT-MAJOR: Now we have to sort something out!
Listen…
I confess I came along with Himanen
to meet you!

ELSA: Oh God…*Subtext!*

SERGEANT-MAJOR: I also need your…not
inspiration…but the other thing…
Intuition!
And someone to support me…someone…look
me in the eye…I need….You!

ELSA: What's he doing with her? Backstage is so
dangerous for relationships! Let me go!

SERGEANT-MAJOR: I forbid you to go after the
adolescents!
Start glowing with revolutionary zeal for me!

ELSA: I *do* feel the spirit of that
Revolution…Freedom is always Sexy!
Ooh, ooh, ooh…Where is he!
Come back to me, before my fervour fades!

SERGEANT-MAJOR: When I was lying in bed, full of
envy, beside
the lad…and listened every night to
what he could invent, with a woman like
you around , I imagined…I wished the woman

was there instead of Him!
I imagined you as a stately noble woman
who has fallen from the clouds of heaven to lie
next to me, who just rests somewhere and
breathes the breath of genius into a man!

ELSA: I am the revolution
making him the first to *invent* everything in the world!
My own doctor!

She forgets that it is the SERGEANT-MAJOR she is addressing...

Dry ice... revolutionary banners...
(*She whispers spells to the SERGEANT-MAJOR, not
recognising him.*)
Do you hear me, my doctor? I am the army of
revolution which you lead!
And I am the pack, which
you carry on your back!
And my feminine fervour is that hot wind,
which will fan the flame of revolution
And we, the whole of mankind, can follow!
(*She sees who it is.*)
Is it you there?
But where is the doctor?
Was it you all the time?
Him! What's keeping him?

SERGEANT-MAJOR: How can you chase after an
adolescent...
when a man like me...with his revolutionary firearm...
needs someone exactly like you as
his woman...leave the rascal!

*HIMANEN enters covered all over with whipped cream. ELSA
goes out of her mind with jealousy...*

ELSA: Whipped cream! From that cow!
Off her, that is off her!
And the knees! Look!
The entire Finn philosopher, covered!
Right, I'm out of here!

HIMANEN: Feeling emptier than ever…
  For tomorrow…
  Now I have experienced everything in the world!

ELSA: So…it didn't even involve love!
  That's what it means!
  'Feeling emptier than ever'…that's what that means!
  Surely we know this? Do you know what you are?
  (*She cries.*) The dreams I've dreamed about you and me!

HIMANEN: There won't…there won't be a child I hope…

ELSA: What? What are you saying?
  Now I'm really leaving the show!

HIMANEN: For God's sake, don't go!
  Mother…no; you, how much longer till
  midnight?

ELSA: Did you just call me mother?
  Mother!
  So many people have warned me about this!
  Thank you!
  I see you now as others see you!

HIMANEN: Yes, sure, why bother anymore?

ELSA: (*Clinging firmly to HIMANEN.*) Sorry! Sorry!
  Forget I said that…
  it was just a jealous woman's venom!
  I'm at full steam here? At full steam!

HIMANEN: Is this senile dementia?

ELSA: What did you say?
  You don't look happy
  either!
  What did that person do to you?

HIMANEN: What does tomorrow mean?

ELSA: I've had such a vision…that at night in the
  forest…we dived together in each others arms
  into a spring…where the water was terribly
  cold and clear…so that you could see the

starry sky in it...even from its depths...and
that spring was bottomless! And at last we
arrived at an underground current...where
black swans were nesting and that's why they
were black...and we knew
that though we think we're unhappy...
actually...we are happy!...This doesn't make
any sense...
Did I make it up?

HIMANEN: A couple of hours has passed! Where am I?
A couple of hours!

ELSA: I'll calm down.
You go over there!

HIMANEN goes next to the SERGEANT-MAJOR.

HIMANEN: May I ask one question before we go to sleep?
What's wrong with my salute? What irritates you so
much?

SERGEANT-MAJOR: The bend of the wrist!
When you do it like this...
(*He demonstrates.*)
it is the disabled state...the act of submission.
'Don't come'
You're not pressing your waist enough.
That's where manliness is.
A woman is a vase...she keeps pushing
herself down, to protect the foetus.
A man keeps pushing himself upwards
into a warning triangle.
Look...you have to raise the pressure from
the waist up...put your mind into your waist
and swell like a bull till the steam comes out
of your shoulders!
A bull is pure *chest*...aggressive chest...hardly
any waist or arse at all...just a place to hang a
tail!
Courage is here! (*He points to his neck.*)
What does a woman have in her slender neck
here?

Cunning!
The male is thick here!
Think about the male lion; enormous mane,
jaws, chest and paws, which is attached to the
shoulder for menacing leaps!
Try to imagine being the prey waiting
beneath…keep the pressure in…you must
breathe *out* from your heart and *in* from
your enormous chest…not through the mouth…
the man's mouth is for *blustering with rage*!
A woman pampers her pelvis…a man makes his
suffer!
Try to press it…like this…

He demonstrates. HIMANEN tries to copy…

HIMANEN: Like this? Is this right?

SERGEANT-MAJOR: No, it's all happening in your throat!
It shows on your helpless face!
Is your pelvic area suffering?
Himanen, ill-treat your pelvis like a man!
And then your eyes!
Where are the eyes of a tiger?
Under the brow, deep-set, safe from claws
and hoof in a fight, from the kick of hooves,
facing front, not looking furtively about!
Where are the eyes of a hare?
In the temples!
Right by the ears!
Looking backwards, round-eyed!
Because the hare spends its life trying to find
the escape route!
The more cowardly the creature, the more its
peering round…all the time…like this!
Just like you!
But the tigers, we tigers, lift up your cheeks
like this, use all the flesh on your face to
protect your eyes, here, up, like this, like this.
the eyeball becomes hard, hard as stone, if you train
it! Train, train! Look, like this, poke your eye
with your finger…like this!

(*He pokes his cheekbones, his eyes.*)
Look, my eye never blinks!
Just look at you!

He pokes HIMANEN in the eye.

HIMANEN: Don't! I can't see!

SERGEANT-MAJOR: See how weak your eye is?
Who are you going to kill with those sheep's eyes?
A look can kill you!
Try and kill me!
(*He pokes HIMANEN in the eye again.*)
Look at you, Goddamn it!
Make your cheekbones hard, like this!
Just take a look at this look! (*He looks.*)
Look at it! Look at me!
Now…try to look back!
(*HIMANEN does.*)
No, damn it! Hopeless!
You look like a pig's bum! (*He moulds HIMANEN's face.*)
Heck, these are very loose…

HIMANEN groans. SERGEANT-MAJOR hits him, which HIMANEN dodges.

Look, like this, look at me!
Stand still while I'm helping you!
Stop gulping!
It brings your Adam's apple up!
There it is!
You've got your Adam's apple up!
Having a game with me, are you?
Giving me the runaround are you?
I'd die of shame if somebody said to me my Adam's apple was up!

ELSA goes back to her auditorium seat, starts doing the Guardian crossword…

Your Adam's apple is up!
Say it to me!

HIMANEN: Your Adam's apple is up!

SERGEANT-MAJOR: (*Affecting horror.*) For God's sake!
You've got an Adam's apple like a woman's!
Look at my Adam's apple...look...from the
pelvis up...it has to be put in its place!
Like this, like this, look at me, look now!
Bring it up, bring it up...this is too loose...
from here...through here...up here...and
dammit...up to here!
Now...the eyes!
Cheek muscles taut!
Now, be a tiger, smelling the hot blood of
your prey...anticipating the rapture of
laceration...try grimacing...like this, this...
Like a cruel tiger you tear your victim apart
and now you ravage with your teeth the
struggling, womanlike, hot fugitive flesh of
your prey panting in mortal agony!
Look... the bloodlust curls in the nostrils,
bringing the flesh of the face up, see, see,
so it stares cruelly...because of the prey's
dread.. hahaha...look, now, now!
(*He shows his eyes.*)
The prey's dread makes the eyes go hard with joy,
the gums in the boiling blood, dismembering
the prey in hot blood.
Well, now, try again, by me.
Don't fool about, Goddamn! (*Hits out at HIMANEN.*)
Into Tiger, now!
Useless!
Relax now and pay attention.
The Beast Male, The Man...is A Look.
A Look of Mauling Rapture caused by Blood Lust!
This Kind...
Now you Die, Himanen!
It makes a whole: a threatening entity of eyes,
face muscles, thick neck and above all,
shoulders, stretching out high above the victim!
How do you take the first step when marching?
March!
Goddamn, I guessed as much!
The pelvis totally inert!

You've got to start from the pelvis…
straighten your knee from the pelvis down!
'The foot has to make the journey from the
pelvis down.'
You're marching with your back!
Let the, let the…go on…belch!
It doesn't matter! Chest!
More Chest, goddamn it!

They march themselves into a sweat.

And straighten your knee, now! Like this…
from pelvis down!
Like this!
Chest out…a coward keeps his chest in!
It's the position of the internals!
In them dwells courage!
You get it from there!
All you need is your chest out and you
stop being a coward!
Internals to the correct position!
The blood cannot enter the liver and kidneys
if the chest isn't out!
Out!
Blood into the liver and kidneys!
You don't have a man's voice…listen to you…
Oeoeoeoe…
From here…
Aeaeaeaea…it rolls, do you hear?
It rolls like thunder, like a landslide…like a
falls of the rapids! Listen! As if a stack of
logs were overtoppling! Listen!
Listen!
Try it yourself!…go on try…

HIMANEN tries to adopt a manly voice…

You've no voice either!
(*He hits HIMANEN in the chest.*)
Chest out, or I'll hit you again!
I'll hit your heart till it stops!
A man has chest flesh and muscle on his
front to protect his heart!

Protect your heart!
Growl in anger!
Look, look, Now!
And growl!
The chest can't come forward unless you
give it a push from the coccyx up!
It's a man's nature to have muscles protecting
his heart!
Just as women has fat on the curves round the
pelvic bowl and that has caused the rocking of
the hips, designed surely by the devil himself…!
March, march always from the coccyx up like
a man, not like a woman!
The evolution of the women's pelvic bowl is
that rocking, designed by the devil himself
that rocking in their entire rear equipment,

ELSA gets up to see if this is still going on. It is… back to the
crossword…

those rear cheeks of theirs with dimples in the
side and all the soft white bellies, and under the navel
those, those frizzling, and their serpentines coccyxes,
and, and in their steps and in their entire, tossed
in all directions-rocking in the panties curled bottom,
which is split! Split like an apple!
Partly split, juicily split, a woman is partly split!
Skittle-shaped in her wedding gown!
And on the point of falling on her back…
A bride always fall on her back!
The high-heeled shoes…well, it's obvious…
they help them to fall backwards…onto their
backs…
Something horrifying happens to him.
Erection!
Now, now!
What the hell?
Himanen, turn your back!
He jumps out of bed.
Himanen, stay there!
An erection near a man!
How can I go on living after this?

HIMANEN: But you were talking Dirty! About Women!
Surely that's what did it? Heavy Smut!
It even had an effect on me! Do you understand?

Being Finnish, he unembarrassedly shows his own tumescence…

SERGEANT-MAJOR: Never before in men's company!
I've never before…no, whatever anybody said!
But, how, why do I now…in men's company…
God damn, I went completely round the bend
because of you!
I'm shamed forever in my own eyes!
Shameful individual!
Sound the retreat!

HIMANEN: Of all the possibilities he hits on this…
Stupid man!
English Man!

SERGEANT-MAJOR: Don't you understand,
this constitutes the
loss of credibility of the whole army!?

HIMANEN: Hey…Tomorrow, I'm *nothing*!… Calm down…

SERGEANT-MAJOR: I need to report it immediately to
my superiors! Corroborated sighting of…
'The Homosexual Gene!'

He takes his hanging ropes out…

HIMANEN: Don't play around!

She reluctantly puts down her crossword…

ELSA: Confiscate the rope!
This is what this Sergeant-Major character
has been after all along! Death!
And now he's depressed!
Get me the rope!

SERGEANT-MAJOR: There's never been a single
suggestion before
of this kind of thing!
Now someone dies!

HIMANEN: Look, tomorrow I'm done for
    I don't have time to play around…

SERGEANT-MAJOR: Bastard!
    …after all we've been through!

HIMANEN: I don't care, Gettit!
    You don't exist any more!
    Without me there's no you!

SERGEANT-MAJOR starts beating and strangling HIMANEN
with the hanging rope.

SERGEANT-MAJOR: I made you…so I can destroy you!
    Now!

ELSA: (*Clinging to the SERGEANT-MAJOR.*) Stop, fools!
    Why, this isn't about you two!
    You're looking at each other, but seeing
    someone else!
    When you hit each other, you beat someone
    else!
    Don't kill each other!

SERGEANT-MAJOR: I'll let go of you…as long as you
    don't disturb
    my last moments!
    And you…think of me!
    Think of my life!
    Nothing tawdry during the last moments of
    my life!
    People under a death sentence don't tug or
    pull…
    My apologies to everyone!

HIMANEN: (*Out of his mind…*) Don't, don't… don't leave
    me! Wait till the dawn! Wait until morning!

ELSA: I love you!

She struggles with the SERGEANT-MAJOR until he gets excited
and overcome with emotion.

    And you there, good old man…
    don't you understand…that you've been

written to do this? So its like you're driving yourself,
to follow the cruellest advice from your worst
enemy into a corner from which you can only
escape by self-destruction!

SERGEANT-MAJOR: I get it! You're threatening the very
thing which
made me accomplish everything in my life!
and without which I am nothing! Why would
you want to take a man's role away from him?

ELSA: What you're doing isn't human!
Don't you understand, you've just
been written like this for the stage?
Since there are no differences in class,
no boundaries…nothing is forbidden…since
there is no motivation…there is no art either
there is therefore no role! There is no society!
No theatre portraying the world! Since there
is no society, where all is *role*, there is therefore
no theatre, where the roles are!
I don't have a role, but I have plenty of play!
You have a role, but no play!
You're not a human being…you're a written part!

SERGEANT-MAJOR: What are you saying? That I've
been *written*? Haven't I decided for myself who I am and
what I do?

ELSA: You ask that with a noose around your neck?
Who here has decided himself what kind of role
he has? We are all somebody's
cartoons here!

SERGEANT-MAJOR: You're saying I'm not a human
being?
Answer me!
Am I a human being?

ELSA: You've been written to be a laughing-stock…
and to be my contrast…my opposite!
But I at least know that I suffer the humiliation
of being the creation in lines of someone, who longs
for the limelight!

There, it's said!
There's Art!
That's what art is today!
Yet you, Fool, don't even notice that you've
been written to prove that *Someone* has a
sense of humour, when, actually, they *haven't!*

SERGEANT-MAJOR: I've been *Written?*
Who the hells dares to say I've been *Written?*
You say I've been written...
and not made by *Fucking.* ...I'm not saying that,
I'm not saying that!...some old Finnish codger has
written me out as a self-portrait of himself!

ELSA: And two British women have translated you
and adapted you and put you
here, you daft old cartoon...

SERGEANT-MAJOR: Anyone who claims that this fist is a
portrait, gets it straight in his eye!
I'll run amok!
I'm Real!
Real!
Did I hear someone laugh?
I'm the sort of self-portrait who doesn't let
anyone laugh at me!

ELSA: Prove for us...with all the stupidity he's
characterised you with...how artificial you are...
Follow someone's cynical plot!
Make people laugh at your
stupid, solemn face!

SERGEANT-MAJOR: Well...right...I refuse to do anything
belonging
to this role!
I'll just do what I want!
Down with Art!
Long Live Me!
Out of my own head!
Long live My Whims!
Now...a kingdom of freedom!
If it's a ladies' man you're after...no sweat!

And that thing that makes a man laugh at
Himself...without knowing why...a sense of
Humour...that's it!
And charm!
Paper, quickly, paper! *I'll* do writing as well!
Letters...that's what women really like...
You can use words to show an emotion...!
Here are my emotions!

He is handing out papers to women in the auditorium...

ELSA: Don't open them! Give them to me!
    Good God, anything might be in them!
    Has he just given you one? Don't open it!

SERGEANT-MAJOR: Are you saying I'm full of ink?
    I am blood!
    Blood boiling with the nearness of woman!
    Let me think dirty thoughts about you!
    I'm going to make a completely improper
    suggestion just for the occasion...

He takes out of a bag the uniform of a French maid.

    ...just pop this on!
    ...its got to be either a French
    Maid, or a Country Shepherdess so I can
    get a hard-on!

*KATE CURRENT enters with her lap full of drug packages and
hypodermic syringes in her mouth.*

KATE: Hey, this is your medicine.
    I bring the chemical illusion of freedom
    which is both the allure and disappointment of drugs.
    I'll be over there!

*STAGE MANAGEMENT enter, both have torches and are wearing
Security Firm Uniforms...they search the auditorium for KATE.*

STAGE MANAGEMENT: (*Acting valiantly and badly.*)
    There's been a Drugs Raid!
    The daughter or daughter-in-law or whatever
    of the editor-in-chief is number one Prime Suspect!
    Follow the trail of straw packing...

A big bale of straw moves apparently on its own...

SERGEANT-MAJOR: I have no solidarity with Uniforms
    any more!

*There is a huge fight between him and the security men. The
SERGEANT-MAJOR drives them away, and brings KATE
forward...*

    Girl...I can smell you!
    You're in heat!

ELSA: What if she was your daughter?

SERGEANT-MAJOR: Well, isn't that liberation?...doing
    first what
    nobody would ever do?
    And now, I'll do you, girl!
    I think that's what my character would do!
    Where's the straw?
    The last time I did this, Elvis was alive!

*SERGEANT-MAJOR and KATE go backstage carrying a bale of
straw...*

HIMANEN: Why is he doing that?

ELSA: That's the question...take me and explore
    that paradigm and my paradigm quietly,
    secretly, exhaustively...

Her and HIMANEN exit as...

    I think those two over there will
    be so busy that we could have an
    interval now...if we haven't had one already!

*STAGE-HANDS enter, carrying huge rockets and HIMANEN's
soapbox/lectern. They have not noticed all the deviations from the
script. There is a sound of amplified fucking over the speakers...*

STAGEHAND: Hey, Mike, where are they?
    We were listening over the PA...and we haven't
    heard a line we recognise for yonks!
    Where the hell did they go?

LIGHTING ENGINEER: They are over stage left...the
one from the audience...and (*Names of two playing
SERGEANT-MAJOR and KATE.*) are in the straw
together... doing...well...I needn't spell it out!

Everybody listens to the amplified fucking...

ASM: What's going on? When do they come back on?
What's the cue for The Finn's fireworks then?

LIGHTING ENGINEER: I know nothing! I say nothing!
You're on your own with the firework cue!

ASM: But don't we strike the handbag and the money?

*They take the handbag and money and clutch it to their breasts.
The four actors return.*

SERGEANT-MAJOR: That was like a route-march up
Ben Nevis!
Now, lad, we have to decide...how will we divide
up the women?
Hell, no...dividing up the women is the old text...
All women in the world belong to me, because
I'm The Father!
And whores don't exist any more...
only in my old role's head!
Holy Smoke...we were communicating in the
straw like two roaring sex chat lines!
Lad, lad, look at the straw...it's in shreds!

HIMANEN: What a powerful sensation...as if I had a
lion beating its tail inside me!
Tommy, I wouldn't have known that a woman
can be like a rucksack full of crayfish!
Oh, Imanuel Kant, what a categorical imperative!
And me...
as hard and long as a church wall!
Why, I was on her...
puffing steam, like a stonewall surrounding
a church!

SERGEANT-MAJOR: And why was I frightened of these
whores? I was scared, because I didn't know what they

did when they fall on their backs! Why be afraid,
if you put straw down? Look at the way Tommy Tommo
shreds the straw to smithereens…even with a big
lass between him and it!

The Women enter. ELSA in her nightgown and wearing a
negligee, staggering happily and reaching for support. She tries to
reach the stove, which has been baking a sponge cake since the
interval.

ELSA: I wouldn't have been able to stand…except I
    desperately wanted to come and have a look at
    Himanen's birthday cake!
    I'd like to shout… 'Chase me naked!'
    Goodness, look at you
    lust devouring you like a wolf!
    Sergeant-Major, may I thank you for making a
    man out of Himanen…he has no mercy for a
    woman! …he sends
    a woman back to Nature! No mercy, from
    Himanen, none whatever, I swear!

KATE: The sergeant-major did a hell of a job!
    Very effective as a trainer!
    It's a wonder my bones didn't break!

ELSA: The noise we made! I am like a dancing open
    fireplace! I am like a fountain splattering flames!
    And Himanen comes like a fucking fire engine!
    I thought I was turning into an *orang utang,*
    I was upside down, arse about tit,
    with my feet up over my shoulders!
    When he was whipping me with his egg
    whisk of passion…I was *omelette!*
    He made me change colour like a tropical sunset!

HIMANEN: Nobody told me that a mature woman is
    like mulled wine!

ELSA: You kiss like a bull!
    You showed no mercy…though I'm curling up
    like birchbark in the fire, you're still coming
    at me like a campfire of logs!

KATE: After she's fucked a sergeant-major
a woman feels like she's done fifty laps on a sawdust
track.
Fuck!…the sweat!
All the way round he called out
all the stations from Lands End to John O'Groats,
turned round, and steamed through them all on
the way back!

HIMANEN: Indeed, it appears to me now that those
pre-birthday
fears of mine were foolish in the extreme!
I've got to admit when Himanen comes in,
thighs part!
It's a given…I meet someone, the thighs open!

ELSA: Why wasn't Himanen here right from the beginning
to lead this play and us and the whole country?
Let alone the entire world!
Bring on wondrous costume for me!

The rack of ecru underwear is pushed on…

Fly in a glorious stage design!
Quickly, bring them on, for me!
On stage! And I'll stay! Himanen, I'll die! I'll
die! My sweat is pouring! Thunder is
racking in my sky and a fireball is blazing under
my skirt! My hair is whipping the trees and rocks!
…and the bottom of the lake and the upper regions
of the heavens…and those stars up there…so near you
can hold them in your hand! Was it you who spoke
of senile dementia?…what brought those to mind?
What else is there in the script at the moment…
before we reach The Curtain? And the party after
that! Aren't we having a party as soon
as we've taken the Bow? Let's start it now!

ELSA: Himanen, into the centre! With your soapbox!
Hot Boy, make a speech about me from your
soapbox! To our contemporaries!

HIMANEN: I won't do contemporary debates any more!
I pass!

KATE enters carrying a layer cake…

KATE: I brought a cake…for my engagement to the Finn!
It's a layer cake…it's a metaphor for the multi-textuality
of the piece, yeah?

ELSA: What? What engagement? There's another rewrite
here;
Darling, take the lead!

KATE: But in Julie Goodyear's script we get engaged!

ELSA: You see, this is what happens when Himanen is
not allowed to take the lead! This is what happens
in the play and in the world! Himanen will soon
arrange a funeral for you, and serve it out to the
audience as a funeral tea!

HIMANEN: Now we can bury the middle class, here in
the Soho Theatre! Let them eat cake!

ELSA: Look!

KATE is scratching plaster from the wall…

What have you got in your mouth?

KATE: Plaster! I'm eating the very fabric of society, yeah?

ELSA: That tart is eating plaster out of a brick wall!
Plaster!
Look, my own daughter is eating plaster!
It's the Whipped Cream Woman!
My God…she's pregnant…with my lover's
child!
Sergeant-Major, swear, on your knees…

SERGEANT-MAJOR does so…

SERGEANT-MAJOR: I Sergeant-Major Thompson, swear
that my daughter, in the event something happens to
her, on account of which she cannot be my
daughter, ceases to be my daughter, by such
measures for which I myself alone take full
responsibility!
But this is Murder!

ELSA: If I can't get pregnant by Hot Boy, neither
can she! And no one else either! No one!

SERGEANT-MAJOR: I was confused! I didn't realise I was
taking an oath!
Pregnancy hasn't been confirmed yet
...we're waiting for urinanalysis!
The pee's best in the morning...
Girl...come here...!

ELSA: She ate plaster! She's pregnant!
And you just swore to disappear her!

SERGEANT-MAJOR: It's true...I swore!
Now...how can I...get some water in this bucket...
she'll have to be drowned!

*ASM comes on with water and a bucket. He runs water into a
bucket...*

ELSA: I want that man's child!
Everyone will understand that!
I'll have a whole new life, pregnant...become younger...
reborn along with that child!
What is that nutcase doing now?
Sergeant-Major, you can carry out your oath
after the child is born!

SERGEANT-MAJOR: (*Trying to drown KATE in the bucket.*)
I can't!
(*He pours the water from the bucket on himself.*)
Now, it's the end of the world!
Look, it's raining there just like this!
The Word says...
'Rain fell for forty days and forty nights.'
Ark!
We must build an Ark!
Timber!
The whole family, here! And timber!

A hand loom is brought out.

There is Thompson's Ark.
He shouted 'Family'

Himanen, at last we have a family!
I can't resist birthday parties!
Himanen, I'll decorate a cake for you...with
Twenty-two candles! (*She does...*)

SERGEANT-MAJOR: This is Thompson's Ark!
(*He holds out KATE's panties.*) Hoist Current's panties to
the mast, Himanen! We as a family have to rescue, no
only the world and mankind, but also the animals!
Look, heavens and Heath Robinson! The
animals themselves have come to visit our ark!

HIMANEN: I can see only people who are feeling lonely...
Lonely people who don't see...that others
Care about them and they care about the others!

ELSA: Look...there's a polecat...and over there a
Silver fox! Let's not take them!

SERGEANT-MAJOR: All animals are allowed in the ark!
Now sit still even though the water is rising!
A hot-blooded mare! Sugar for her!

HIMANEN: But it's wearing a ring on its ring finger!
It's someone's wife! How did I become so
genital that even the animals look like human
Beings? Don't!

SERGEANT-MAJOR: Whooper Swan!

HIMANEN: I think it's a Finnair air hostess!

SERGEANT-MAJOR: Swans always make me burst into tears!
That song...'Upon the washing of its plumes,
lifts up the pure breast again'! I always start
weeping there...wondering what kind of breast
will lift up pure...Hold on to me...it is
so soporifically soft! Don't let me start
plucking...

HIMANEN: Now, the funeral of middle class values will
begin
here in the auditorium of The Soho Theatre
In honour of my birthday! Dear
grieving Middle Class England! Friends

and Loved Ones! My funeral speech is short…
the mothers of the young will get what they want!'

ELSA: Middle Class England, this cake is your body,
and this water shed from my eye is your blood,
which is given for you to the audience.
(*She begins to cut the cake.*)
Oops…what's in it…a cherry stone…something
hard…ooops…what…what can it be…A gun…

SERGEANT-MAJOR: Wait a minute!…A gun, God
damn…this can't be…what's it doing in the cake…

ELSA: A saw blade…Good lord…and a file!

HIMANEN: What an apt image!
I'll announce a new class!
A new Aristocracy…we the people of
the Limelight!
And we, its elite, the aristocrats of aristocrats,
philosophers…The First Ones! It's known
by its uncompromising courage!
Citizens, burn down your theatre…
Break off all contact with Me and this woman
here, because it's her I love!
Love needs enemies! Not friends!
Not approval! It needs persecution and pain!
Hatred and punishment…

ELSA: I understand…and I love you like a She-wolf!
Shall we give a public demonstration?
Here in front of everyone?

HIMANEN: I'll get engaged to you!
Without rings!

ELSA: And so that the inhabitants of this place
will sever all contact with us…
and no one will offer a single word of congratulation…
The Sergeant-Major can weave us engagement
rings made out of each other's pubic hair!

The SERGEANT-MAJOR pulls pubic hair out of each of their crotches. Shrieks.

SERGEANT-MAJOR: If only I could see!
 Here are tassles of real silk!
 I just wish I could see!

ELSA: (*They exchange rings.*) This love blazes,
 if only it's persecuted enough!
 Hate us and you'll make this love last forever!
 Was it you who said to me… 'If this is
 senile dementia…'?

The swan glides across the back…ELSA sees it…

 Himanen…it suddenly strikes me…
 whether all this love is not just the dream of
 a dying woman!
 Are you real, Himanen?
 Are you just a trick of the light?
 If I'm just a terminal care patient…and
 you've all been watching from the side…
 when I've just been raving about love and
 the ardour of life…and I'm just about to slip
 over to the other side!
 You are looking strangely at me!
 Why is Metaphor Girl crying?

KATE: Because you're not the chief editor of a
 big important newspaper at all.
 You just deliver newspapers.
 And you've slipped during your nightly round
 and hit your head…
 celebratory fireworks sound and light effect…
 and while you were lying
 there unconscious…you developed pneumonia!

ELSA: Am I just a newspaper deliverer?
 Not a big important editor at all?

KATE: You were thrown out of hospital, on the streets,
 to die, like normal these days…because of
 cutbacks…I took pity on you, a stranger, and
 took you home with me to die.

Twenty-two candles light…elsewhere, it is getting dark…

ELSA: Is that my birthday present?
    Eviction and out on the streets?
    Is this what I got?
    Is Himanen the real Himanen after all?
    Now I'm beginning to have doubts…
    is he my only son just got out of jail?
    Who I dream…who in fear of death and not
    being loved I imagine to be Himanen?
    Oh what bad luck…
    to think I was so full of love…and it was
    just the fear of dying!
    Is that it…that love is pure death after all?
    You talk about love because you can't
    talk about death!
    I have a strange feeling…that I prepared this
    cake! For a funeral!
    Don't tell me, this is *my* funeral tea?
    Well, then that proves it…then this *must* be
    the real Himanen!

KATE shakes her head.

    And I wonder, if that's
    definite…whether I'm not the real editor of
    a big newspaper after all!

KATE shakes her head again.

    At least I'm engaged
    to this Himanen!

KATE looks away.

    Now, I have a role…but my
    play will end! Remember all of you, what role you
    play doesn't matter…but everybody only gets one
    play…which ends too soon!

KATE looks at others, embarrassed…

    Now I remember…I was watching this performance.
    But that's impossible, isn't it…I couldn't have
    strolled into the auditorium of the Soho theatre

wearing my nightie! And where's my handbag?
You're just trying to calm me down, Himanen,
so I won't be afraid of death…
and it's changed within me into love for you!
This ecstasy of love is death turned on its head.
Oh, I wish it were midnight already…
so I could give you my present!

Fireworks go off in the vestibule…as the actors…

HIMANEN: Midnight! The Legend Dies!

ELSA: Happy Birthday! Happy Birthday!

Everybody cries 'Happy Birthday'.

HIMANEN: Twenty-two years old.
Proof Positive that the World belongs to
The Young!

*STAGE CREW comes on and begin to strike the
set…muttering…tomorrow's another day…Strike The Set…The
bed goes first…etc.*

ELSA: Are we now in the backyard?
now I'll blow the candles out…and then I…(*Blows.*)

SERGEANT-MAJOR: Off we go…

KATE: This is too sad to watch…

*KATE, SERGEANT-MAJOR and HIMANEN go off, coming
visibly off-duty, off-acting…as…*

ELSA: Don't go. Let's not do the end! We won't perform
it…tell them, my…
Now I see something I've never realised before!
Everything ends.
Things happen at the wrong time.
People go.
It's too late.
We love.

*ASM comes on. Wants to lock up. She kindly lights a last rocket
as…*

There's sound and light and strangeness.
Things go on behind our backs.

The rocket flies up in a blaze of light…

We're all dying.

A large stuffed swan falls from the flies…

Lights out.

The End.

www.ingramcontent.com/pod-product-compliance
Ingram Content Group UK Ltd.
Pitfield, Milton Keynes, MK11 3LW, UK
UKHW020724280225
455688UK00012B/490